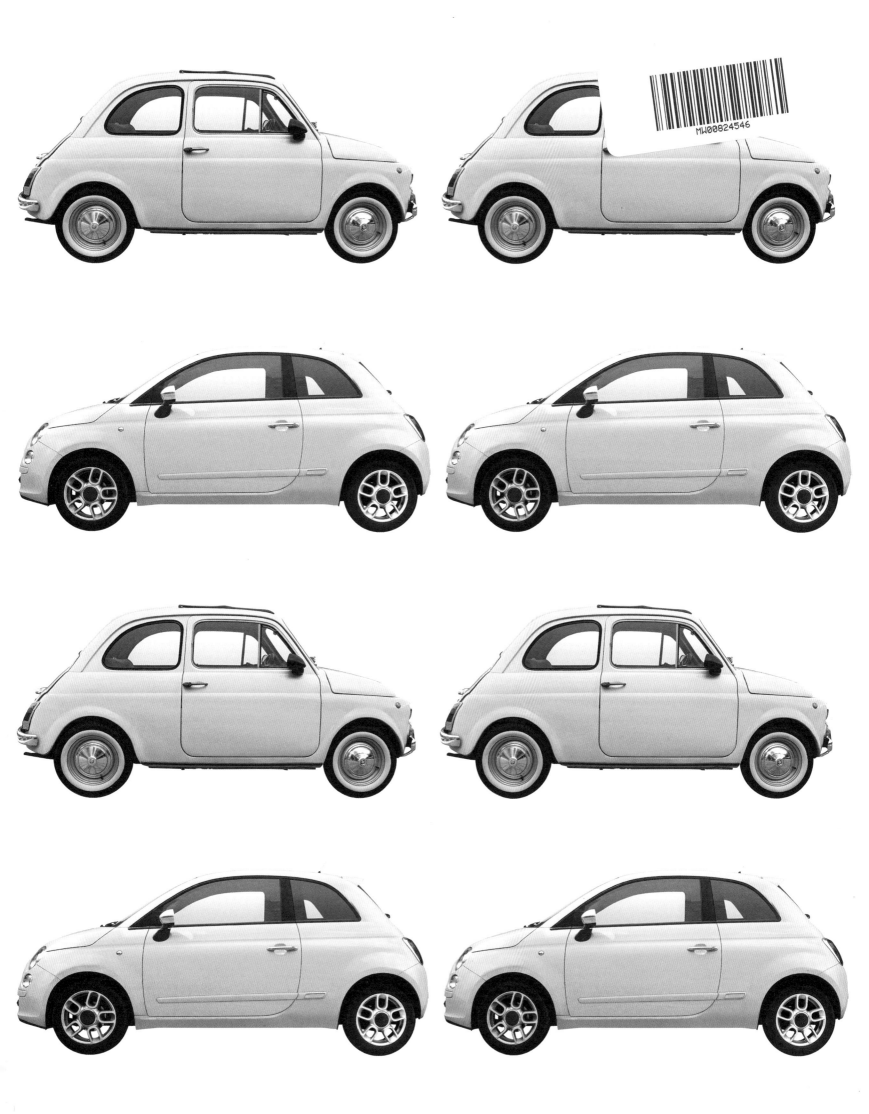

500 FIAT

THE HISTORY OF A LEGEND FROM 1936 TO THE PRESENT

MASSIMO CONDOLO

WHITE STAR PUBLISHERS

Contents

Introduction

Few other cars in the world are as famous, iconic, and far-reaching as the Fiat 500 has been. From winning the Compasso d'Oro to becoming a smash hit in cartoons, it is as much at home in a factory worker's garage as it is in an elegant villa in the hills. Only a few cars have been loved as much as 500s have, both by their owners and by those who gaze at them affectionately as they drive by. None, however, has so universally represented Italian style in the world and, above all, none has been able to repeat all the successes that the 500 achieved with three completely different models created from 1936 to 2007, including the quintessential "modello 110" born in 1957. Even its derivatives and substitutes that were less fortunately perceived, such as the 126 of the '70s and the Cinquecento and Seicento of the '90s, profited from the aura of their ancestors and reached sales of millions of units. Because in all of its versions, the 500 is and always has been the car of European people, even before concepts like "world car" and "car of the people" were invented.

4-5 THE 1957 500 UNVEILS ITS HEIR: A HIGHLY EFFECTIVE GIMMICK CREATED WITH AN ELASTICIZED CAR COVER TO PRESENT THE 2007 MODEL.

6-7 "THE FOUNDERS OF F.I.A.T.," PAINTED BY LORENZO DELLEANI, DEPICTS THE MEETING HELD ON JULY 1, 1899. EMANUELE CACHERANO DI BRICHERASIO IS FIFTH FROM LEFT, AND GIOVANNI AGNELLI IS SEVENTH.

The 500 before the 500: the Topolino

Manufacturing a small car that would motorize the country's population had been in Fiat's DNA since the time the company was founded. Count Emanuele Cacherano di Bricherasio was nicknamed the "Red Count" because of his progressive ideas, which included the concept that motorizing the population would be an instrument of emancipation. He had gathered a group of noteworthy citizens that included noblemen and industry captains around him in the hopes of persuading them to build an auto industry; and after countless meetings at the Caffè Brunetto, near Turin's Porta Nuova station, an encounter was arranged on July 1, 1899 at his family palace in Via Lagrange 20. The participants were the founding members of Fiat Automobiles, whose incorporation deed was registered ten days later and included the senator Giovanni Agnelli and the entrepreneur Giovanni Battista Ceirano. The first Fiat model, the 3½ HP, descended from Ceirano's Welleyes, designed by Aristide Faccioli.

7 THE FIAT FACTORY ON THE CORNER OF CORSO DANTE AND CORSO MASSIMO D'AZEGLIO IN TURIN. THE 1915 PROTOTYPE WAS BUILT HERE, THE VERY FIRST AUTOMOBILE TO BE CALLED FIAT 500.

Fiat

But the first Fiat was small because of the limits of Italian industry at the time and not because of Bricherasio's ideals, which he didn't live long enough to see implemented. During the war with Libya, Fiat was busy supplying war machinery and vehicles, but when the war in Libya was over, the company technicians went back to designing a small car that would be mass-produced, just as the Oldsmobile Curved Dash and the Ford Model T were being produced on the other side of the Atlantic. The 1915 prototype was compact and open, with two seats and a four-cylinder, 500 cc engine, but the project was abandoned during World War I. When the war was over, it was decided that the project would be unable to withstand the competition of the cyclecars (lightweight vehicles with little more than motorcycle mechanics) available on the French and English markets that were perfect for such a model. Italy's economic structure was not ready for a truly working-class car yet. Fiat did not venture into that market segment until 1925, when it produced the 509 in a variety of utility versions that attracted small and medium enterprises. But the list price of 18,500 lire was still too high for the car to be popular among working-class people. Unconfirmed reports say that Mussolini asked Senator Agnelli for a car that cost only 5,000 lire, a price that was affordable for the middle class. The same reports say that the request was repeated in 1932, when the Balilla 508 was presented; but although its list price of 10,800 lire was significantly lower because of remarkable simplifications in its construction, it was still too expensive except for an elite few.

In any case, Fiat decided to begin constructing an economy car, for Italians as well as for export markets such as France and United Kingdom, where the success of the cyclecars had begun setting the pace. Fiat management identified two parallel but technically opposite strategies for lowering costs: the simplification of traditional techniques, and the design of completely new production processes. This second task was entrusted to Oreste Lardone, a designer mentored by Giulio Cesare Cappa when they worked together at Fiat from 1909 to 1924 and whom he followed to Itala, a company founded by Matteo Ceirano. Lardone began work again on an idea he had developed at Itala with a prototype of a front-wheel-drive compact car that Mario Revelli di Beaumont helped design. The prototype had four seats and an air-cooled engine, and was ready to be tested by 1931, but on the drive up to the Cavoretto hill, on a new road designed for cars and inaugurated in 1928, the prototype, with Agnelli and Lardone test-driving, caught fire. The fire was caused by a simple fuel leak, but Agnelli was convinced that the front-wheel drive was responsible, so he prohibited the use of that technology in any future Fiat vehicles and fired Lardone. The company was left with the first strategy—that of simplifying traditional techniques, which was assigned to the engineers who had created the Balilla: Antonio Fessia, who worked for Fiat from 1925 to 1946, then for NSU-Fiat and then for Lancia, and Tranquillo Zerbi.

8 TWO VERSIONS OF THE 500 (THE TORPEDO ON TOP AND THE COUPÉ DE VILLE ON THE BOTTOM) DESIGNED IN 1915, WHICH NEVER MADE IT BEYOND THE PROTOTYPE PHASE. THE ONLY ONE PORTRAYED IN A NON-RETOUCHED PHOTO IS A TORPEDO, PROBABLY THE ONLY ONE EVER BUILT.

9 TOP A FIAT 501 TORPEDO (1919-1926) AS IT LEAVES CORSO DANTE, THE FACTORY WHERE FIAT'S FIRST MASS-PRODUCED SERIES, THE ZERO, WAS MANUFACTURED.

9 BOTTOM THE FRONT-WHEEL-DRIVE 500, DESIGNED BY ORESTE LARDONE IN 1931. IT CAUGHT FIRE DURING ITS TEST DRIVE, WITH GIOVANNI AGNELLI ON BOARD.

10 THE FIRST TOPOLINO, THE 1934 "ZERO A," DESIGNED BY DANTE GIACOSA (TOP); AND THE SECOND PROTOTYPE (BOTTOM).

11 DANTE GIACOSA PORTRAYED WITH A STANDARD 500, WHICH WAS FIRST PRODUCED IN THE SUMMER OF 1936. THE PROJECT WAS ASSIGNED TO HIM BY ANTONIO FESSIA AND TRANQUILLO ZERBI.
IT WAS THE FIRST TIME HE HAD DESIGNED AN ENTIRE CAR.

Fessia and Zerbi entrusted the project, named "Zero A," to Dante Giacosa, an engineer who had worked with Fessia at Spa, a company that was also founded by Matteo Ceirano and subsequently became part of Fiat. Like his mentors, Giacosa had worked on developing airplane motors; this was the first time he would direct the development of a completely new automobile. His experience in aeronautics influenced the new vehicle's weight distribution and lines, which had been designed by Rodolfo Schaeffer, director of bodywork production. The motor was a small, 569 cc four-cylinder engine with side valves (a solution that made it possible to reduce the height of the car) that reached a power output of 13 HP at 4,000 rpm. Schaeffer's design conditioned the layout of the automobile's internal components. The front-mounted engine was located just in front of the front axle, making it necessary to put the radiator behind the engine, rather than in the usual position. The front wheels were independent, and to reduce the weight of the car, the rear suspension had two quarter-elliptical rather than semi-elliptical springs. The engine, the transmission, the suspension with quarter-elliptical springs, and a crankcase that left space on the sides were all designed to make the transition to a front-wheel-drive version possible without making major changes. In fact, Fessia and Zerbi, as well as

Giacosa himself, considered Lardone's solution to be the best one, but they had to comply with Senator Agnelli's ban on the use of front-wheel-drive systems. In order to simplify and lighten the structure, the body worked together structurally with the frame, which was made of two metal struts with no rear-axle overhang. There was no water pump; a thermosyphon cooling system was used for circulation, and the hot water naturally rose to the top. Nor was there a fuel pump, since there was a gravity-feed carburetor. The engine had a splash lubrication system; the only function of the oil pump was to regulate the flow; it did not pressurize the oil. The 15-inch wheels, produced specifically by Pirelli, were a size that had never been seen on the market before. The Zero A prototype hit the streets in the Canavese area on October 7, 1934, piloted by Giacosa and Fessia, whose family was from the region. They drove a circuit from Turin to Ivrea, beyond the Serra Moraine, down to Vestigné, and from here along the plains to Cigliano and the Turin–Milan highway. The itinerary covered paved and unpaved roads as well as the highway, where the 500 reached a speed of 51 miles per hour (82 kph). The first Zero A, with its small interior and completely recessed headlights, was followed by another model with slightly protruding headlights and an interior that would become more or less the definitive one.

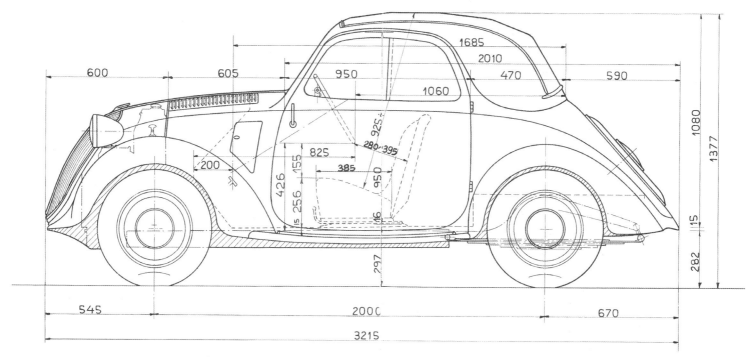

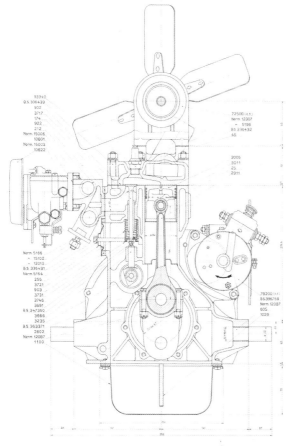

12 TOP THE DRAWINGS ON THIS PAGE ARE OF A CONVERTIBLE 500, FIRST PROPOSED IN THE AUTUMN OF 1936. IT COST 850 ITL MORE THAN THE SEDAN, AND ITS REAR WINDOW WAS PART OF THE CONVERTIBLE TOP.

12 BOTTOM ON THE LEFT, A CROSS SECTION OF THE ENGINE HIGHLIGHTS HOW SIDE VALVES MADE IT POSSIBLE TO LIMIT THE HEIGHT OF THE ENGINE.

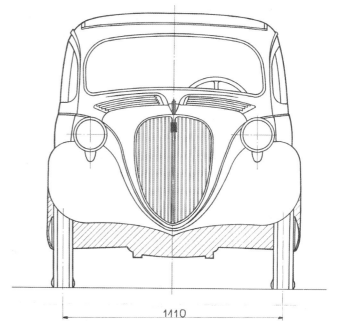

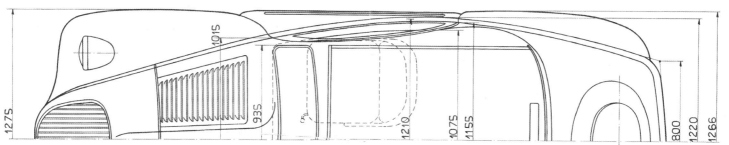

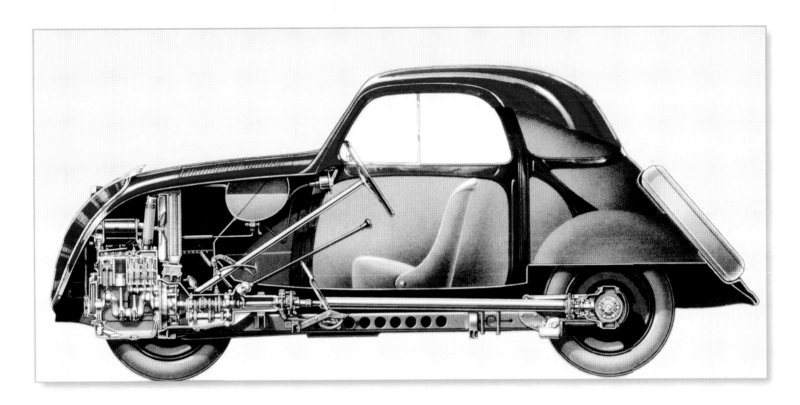

On June 10, 1936, the 500 was presented to the authorities and the press at Villa Torlonia in Rome, the same place where the Balilla had been introduced, using the launch slogan "The small car for working and for saving." Angelo Tito Anselmi, automotive historian, said that the Topolino was "an extraordinary example of auto engineering, a moving episode of the design of an object that had never before existed in that form." Standard equipment included a two-tone finish (the fenders and running boards were always black). Unlike the prototype, the car's headlights were mounted on the fenders with brackets; their resemblance to the round ears of Mickey Mouse led to the nickname "Topolino," the Italian name of the Disney character. It seems that Fiat wanted the nickname to become the car's official name, but the U.S. decided against it because of the diplomatic relations between the two countires, which were not good at the time. In fact, until July 1936, Italy was under sanctions from the League of Nations (today's UN) because of its attack on Ethiopia. Its 8,900-lire price tag (much higher than its original target price of 5,000) was the equivalent of about twenty months of a laborer's average salary, making it the first real economy car in Italy and in Europe. The convertible version that was added to the line had a top that opened as far as the base of the rear window. At 9,750 lire, it was a bit more expensive than the sedan but was in high demand. At the same time it was launched in Italy, the Topolino was also introduced in France, with the brand name Simca (Société Industrielle de Mécanique et Carrosserie Automobile) and the model name Cinq (Five), which indicated its 5 HP taxation class. The Cinq was the first Simca without the Fiat trademark and it was an exact clone of the Italian model, despite being produced by Simca in Nanterre, a northwestern suburb of Paris, using many local components. Simca had been founded by Enrico Teodoro Pigozzi from two previous companies, Fiat-France and Safaf (Société Anonyme Française des Automobiles Fiat), and was already producing the 6 HP (Balilla) and the 11 HP (Ardita). Even in France, the home of the cyclecar, the Topolino was the first real working-class vehicle. Pigozzi's entrepreneurial dynamism was evident in the Cinq's remarkable advertising campaign. The ads underlined that the project to produce a car for the working class was a reality in France, contrary to what was happening beyond the Rhine, in Germany, where Volkswagen had begun taking orders for mass-produced vehicles for the civilian market but would not begin producing them until after the war.

13 A CUTAWAY DRAWING OF THE DEFINITIVE VERSION OF THE 500. THE FRAME HAS NO REAR OVERHANG; IT ENDS AT THE LEVEL OF THE DRIVE AXLE, TO WHICH IT IS CONNECTED WITH A HALF-LEAF SPRING THAT IS NOT VISIBLE.

14-15 THE CLASSIC TWO-TONED, CLOSED-ROOF VERSION OF THE 500
THAT PAOLO CONTE SANG ABOUT IN HIS 1975 JAZZ HIT "LA TOPOLINO
AMARANTO," WHICH NARRATED POSTWAR LIFE.

15 THE ENGINE COMPARTMENT OF THE 500 WITH THE RADIATOR PLACED
BEHIND THE ENGINE RATHER THAN IN FRONT OF IT, MAKING THE LOW,
STREAMLINED HOOD DESIGNED BY RODOLFO SCHAEFFER POSSIBLE.

16 A ROW OF SIMCA CINQS LINED UP IN FRONT OF A FRENCH DEALERSHIP. IN FRANCE, THE PUBLICITY CAMPAIGN FOR THE LAUNCH OF THE 500, PRODUCED UNDER LICENSE, WAS IMPRESSIVE.

17 AN ADVERTISING POSTER FOR THE SIMCA CINQ, SEEN HERE WITH AN OPTIONAL SPLIT BUMPER. THE CAR WAS PRESENTED IN FRANCE AND ITALY AT THE SAME TIME, THANKS TO A SMALL NUMBER OF UNITS MANUFACTURED IN TURIN BEFORE THE PRODUCTION LINES IN NANTERRE WERE COMPLETED.

18-19 A POSTWAR 500 PARTICIPATING IN THE WELSH RALLY, WHICH RESUMED IN 1950 AFTER IT HAD BEEN STOPPED DURING THE WAR. THE BODY WAS PAINTED ONE-TONED LIVERY AND THE BUMPERS HAD NO ROSTRUMS. THE FOUR SEATER, WITH A LONGER BACK ROOF, WAS ALSO AVAILABLE IN THE U.K.

19 TOP A CONVERTIBLE 500 THAT WAS ADDED TO THE CATALOGUE IN 1936, WITH ONE MODEL. ONE OF THE GOALS OF THE 500 PROJECT WAS TO ENTICE THE FEMALE POPULATION INTO THE WORLD OF CARS.

19 BOTTOM A POSTWAR MONOCHROME 500. FENDERS THAT MATCHED THE BODY WERE INTRODUCED IN 1946 WHEN PRODUCTION RESUMED AFTER THE WAR.

FIAT 500 LA VETTURA E IL FU

GONCINO UTILITARI

For fifty days, a Cinq traveled the streets of Paris, nonstop at a pace of 620 miles (1,000 km) a day, registering an average consumption of 0.8 gallons (3.1 l) per 62 miles (100 km). Its mileage capabilities were challenged again in the "Concours du bidon de cinq litres" or the "five-liter can contest" where five Cinqs won the first 5 places in the competition to see which cars would travel the farthest with 1.3 gallons (5 l) of fuel in their gas tanks. During the 1,600 miles (2,600 km) roundtrip Paris-Madrid race, the French Topolino got an average mileage of 0.9 gallons (3.6 l) per 62 miles (100 km), demonstrating once again how thrifty it could be. On the Autodrome de Montlhéry racetrack, a little Cinq reached an average speed of 65 miles per hour (105 kph). After just a few months, a convertible was added to the line. The version was proposed in three trim levels: Standard, Grand Luxe, and Superluxe, and was an immediate success. In the United Kingdom, where the body for the four-seater version was designed, a modification was made to the roof in the back in order to comfortably accommodate two passengers in the rear seat.

22–23 BODY FINISHING AT THE FIAT LINGOTTO IN TURIN, THE FIRST ITALIAN FACTORY WITH A FORD ASSEMBLY LINE. THE ENGINES HAVE NOT BEEN MOUNTED YET.

23 A 500 ROLLS OFF THE ASSEMBLY LINE. TO FACILITATE ENGINE INSTALLATION, THE CARS MOVED ON A SUSPENDED TRACK APPROXIMATELY 3 FEET (1 M) ABOVE THE FLOOR.

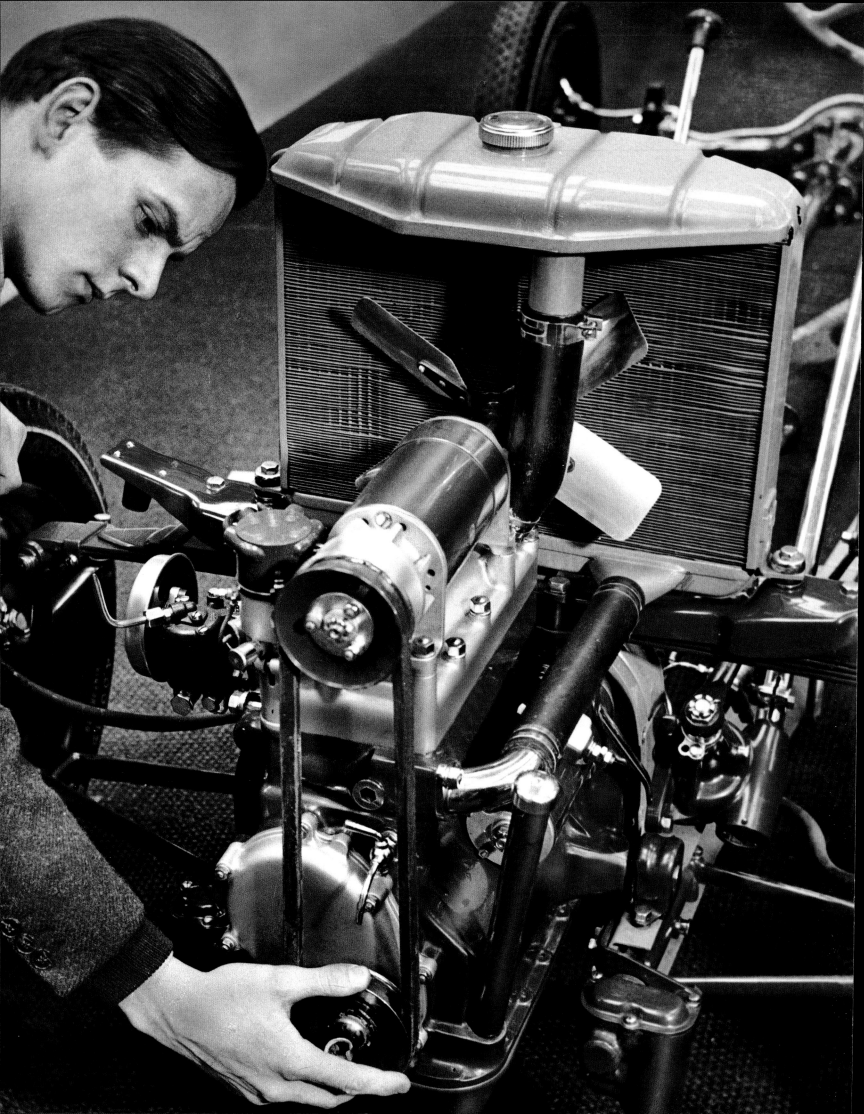

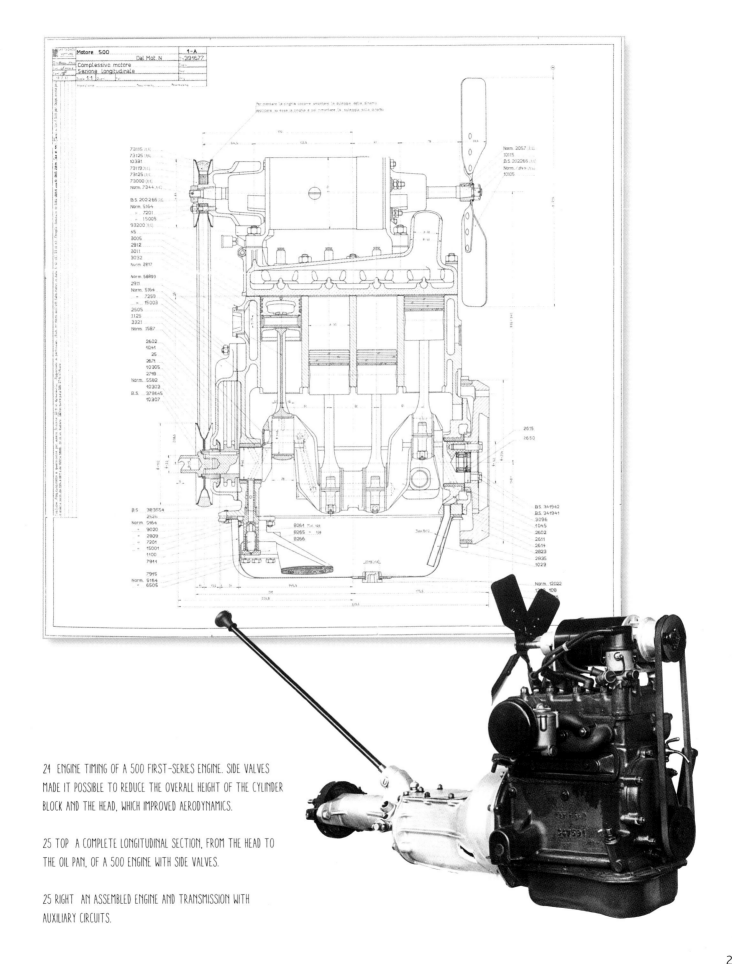

24 ENGINE TIMING OF A 500 FIRST-SERIES ENGINE. SIDE VALVES MADE IT POSSIBLE TO REDUCE THE OVERALL HEIGHT OF THE CYLINDER BLOCK AND THE HEAD, WHICH IMPROVED AERODYNAMICS.

25 TOP A COMPLETE LONGITUDINAL SECTION, FROM THE HEAD TO THE OIL PAN, OF A 500 ENGINE WITH SIDE VALVES.

25 RIGHT AN ASSEMBLED ENGINE AND TRANSMISSION WITH AUXILIARY CIRCUITS.

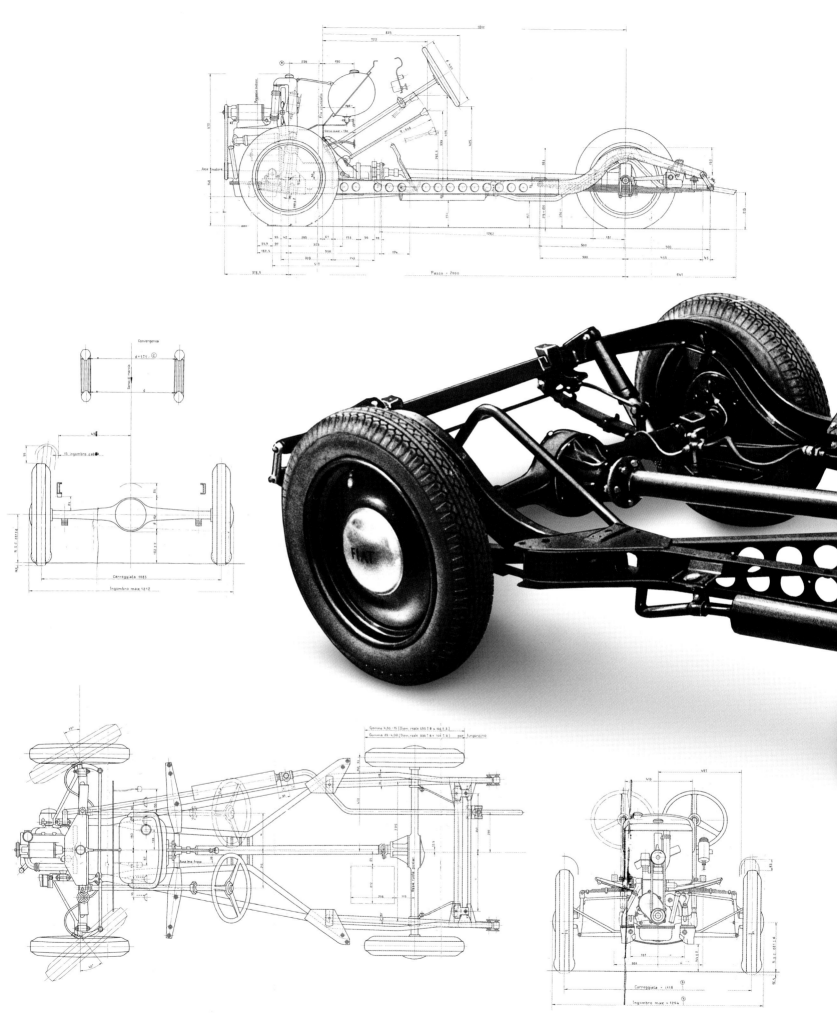

26

26 FRONT, BACK, SIDE, AND PLAN VIEWS OF A 500 "LONG LEAF SPRING" CHASSIS WITH LOWERED LONGITUDINAL MEMBERS THAT CROSS THE REAR AXLE TO REACH THE REAR CROSSBAR.

26-27 THE CHASSIS OF THE "LONG LEAF SPRING" 500 WAS MADE LONGER IN THE BACK TO ACCOMMODATE A SEMI-ELLIPTICAL LEAF SPRING THAT HAD TO BE SHACKLED DOWNLINE OF THE REAR DRIVE AXLE.

28-29 THE 500 VAN WITH A LONG LEAF SPRING ALREADY EXISTED; IT WAS A VERSION CREATED IN 1938 SPECIFICALLY TO ADAPT TO THIS FEATURE. THE SERIAL NUMBER OF THE FIRST CHASSIS THAT ADOPTED IT WAS 46001.

29 AN ILLUSTRATION FROM 1936 FOR THE CATALOG OF THE 500 FURGONCINO, CREATED THAT YEAR ON A SHORT LEAF SPRING FRAME. THE CARGO COMPARTMENT WAS ACCESSED VIA A REAR SWING DOOR.

In 1936, in Italy, production began on the van version, which was available on the price list but was primarily destined for the Royal Army. Beginning in 1937, traffic laws required that closed-body cars be equipped with trafficators, mechanical arms mounted on the windshield struts in the 500, that swung out horizontally to indicate that a turn was about to be made, as well as a taillight group that included parking lights and turn-signal lights. The quarter-elliptical spring suspension created a few problems when the vehicle had to stand up to rough military use, so in 1938 the springs were substituted with more traditional semi-elliptical springs. The modification made it necessary to redesign the back section of the frame, which once again became completely loadbearing as it had been in previous models (with a U-bend that allowed it to straddle the rear axle, similar to buses) and to give up the collaboration between the frame and the body. Since it would not have been convenient to set up another production line specifically for the limited amount of vans that were being produced, beginning with frame 46001, halfway through the year, this modification was applied to all Topolinos, regardless of their body type. The first evolution, one that purists would call a de-evolution, produced the "long leaf spring 500" that weighed 66 pound (30 kg) more than its predecessor. Simca also produced a small, 551-pound-capacity (250 kg) van that was extensively used by the postal system. Its dark green color became a familiar element in France's landscape.

It was also in 1937 that production of the Topolino began in Germany, using the Heilbronn plant

built in 1927 for NSU Motorenwerke. NSU produced motorcycles but wanted to begin building cars; when its project failed, Fiat bought the plant in 1929 and began producing clones of the Italian models with the NSU-Fiat trademark. In 1938, Fiat also acquired the car-body builder Karrosseriewerke Weinsberg, or KW, from the Eisenlohr family, who left Germany due to their difference in opinion with the Nazi government. Although KW remained the property of Fiat until 1970, it operated independently, with commissions that included producing the body of the Kübelwagen (the military version of the Beetle) for Volkswagen, fuselages for Messerschmitt, and truck cabs for Büssing, as well as painting bodies for Porsche. Its two workshops also produced various versions of the NSU-Fiat 500 roadster, which were stylistically very advanced. The 500 was assembled by the Steyr-Puch in Austria, as well as in Warsaw, not at the Państwowe Zakłady Inżynierii (State Engineering Works) where in 1931 Polski Fiat had started producing licensed models, but at its branch in Sapieżyńska Street. Unlike the 508, the 518, and the 618 truck that were produced with some local components, the 500s were sent from Turin unassembled, allowing them to be branded Fiat rather than Polski Fiat. The war brought the production of the Topolino to a halt nearly everywhere. In Italy, the versions produced were almost exclusively public and military vehicles; Simca ceased production after Italy attacked France; NSU-Fiat was busy with military commissions (which included production of the Topolino for the Wehrmacht); and Fiat's Warsaw branch was so violently bombed by German troops that it had to stop production in 1940.

Giacosa designed a battery-operated electric 500, controlled with a trolleybus rheostat, that he used to travel from the office to the temporary housing provided for evacuated Fiat workers, in the hills of Moncalieri.

When production began again in Italy in 1946, the 500s that came off the line were a solid color, with no contrasting colors on the running boards or fenders. Production also resumed in Nanterre, while the disastrous conditions in post-war Germany slowed production in Heilbronn, which did not begin again until 1951. Polski Fiat, on the other hand, never re-opened.

30 AND 30-31 A BEAUTIFUL TWO-SEATER ROADSTER VERSION OF THE NSU/FIAT 500 WAS PRODUCED IN 1939 BY KARROSSERIEWERKE WEINSBERG, A COMPANY THAT FIAT HAD PURCHASED THAT YEAR AND THAT THEY WOULD OWN UNTIL 1970. THE GRILLE WAS THE SAME AS THAT OF THE ITALIAN 500, DESIGNED BY SCHAEFFER.

31 THE ASSEMBLY LINE AT THE FIAT PLANT IN SAPIEŻYŃSKA STREET IN WARSAW. SINCE THEY WERE PRODUCED IN THIS FACTORY AND NOT AT POLSKI FIAT, THE 500S, WHICH ARRIVED UNASSEMBLED FROM ITALY, BORE THE FIAT BRAND. THE PLANT WAS DESTROYED DURING WORLD WAR II BOMBARDMENTS AND NEVER REOPENED.

The last year of the 500 with a side-valve engine was 1947, when production reached 110,000 in Italy and 46,500 in France. In 1948, production began on the 500 B, which was esthetically identical to the first series but had an overhead-valve engine. The engine size of 569 cc remained the same; but the engine, fed by a fuel pump, was more powerful (16 HP at 4,400 rpm) and could reach a speed of 59 miles per hour (95 kph). New features included a two-spoke steering wheel, new dashboard instruments, all beige plastic elements, a fuel

gauge (absent in previous models), and a heater (which was optional.) The frame had four telescopic shock absorbers connected to the wheels and the rear-axle torsion bar. Another version was added to the cargo van, the Giardiniera, a four-seater with a folding rear seat that could transport both cargo and passengers. With ash wood structures and Masonite panels on its sides and doors, it became the first mass-produced "woody." The model was developed from the design by Mario Revelli di Beaumont for Viotti bodyworks,

which he patented with the name Giardinetta. Built by Carrozzerie Speciali (a department of the Lingotto Factory), it had a metallic finish. Its wood panels were varnished with clear gloss, and metal bumpers were standard equipment. The French production began using the new mechanics a year before esthetic renewal would produce the 500 C in Italy. The Six, which replaced the Cinq, had an American-looking front end, but that would not be enough to save it. In 1950, after manufacturing 6,035 of them, production ceased because the model was unable to stand up to the competition of the French four-door models, the Citroën 2CV and the Renault 4CV, with a rear-mounted engine and rear traction. The corporate changes made in Simca that played a role in abandoning production of the Six in 1950 would also lead the company to suspend production of the Fiat clones in favor of the models they resumed producing following a merger with Ford France. The 500 B was eliminated from Fiat's Italian catalogue in mid-1949, after producing 21,000 cars that included sedans (convertibles), Giardinieras, and vans.

32-33 THE 1952 500 C BELVEDERE WITH SHEET-METAL SIDE PANELS REMINISCENT OF THE WOODEN PANELS OF THE GIARDINIERA.

33 TOP THE GIARDINIERA, FIRST MANUFACTURED IN 1947 USING THE B, WAS FOLLOWED BY A C-BASED MODEL, WHICH WAS PRODUCED UNTIL 1952. WITH ASH PILLARS AND MASONITE PANELS, IT WAS THE FIRST MASS-PRODUCED "WOODY."

33 BOTTOM 500 CS ON THE FRATELLI ELIA FIAT 680N VIBERTI CAR-CARRIER THAT TRANSPORTED THEM IN TWO PARALLEL ROWS.

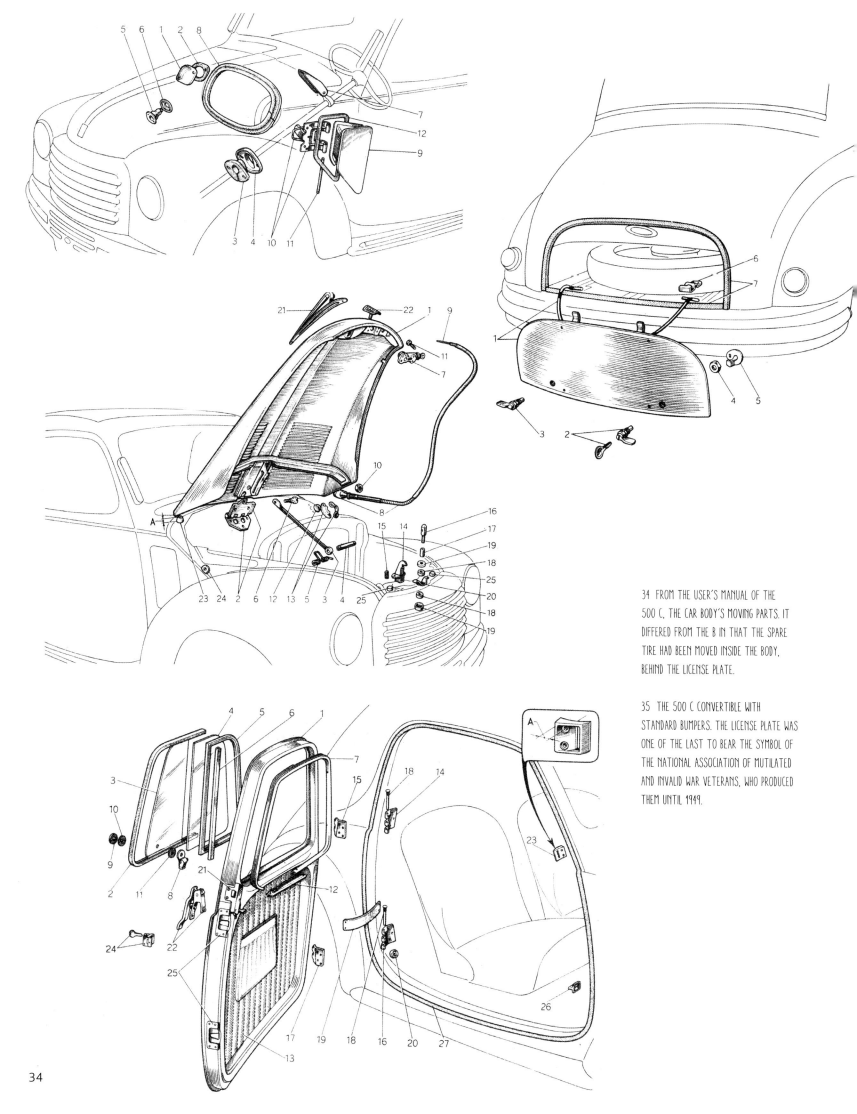

34 FROM THE USER'S MANUAL OF THE 500 C, THE CAR BODY'S MOVING PARTS. IT DIFFERED FROM THE B IN THAT THE SPARE TIRE HAD BEEN MOVED INSIDE THE BODY, BEHIND THE LICENSE PLATE.

35 THE 500 C CONVERTIBLE WITH STANDARD BUMPERS. THE LICENSE PLATE WAS ONE OF THE LAST TO BEAR THE SYMBOL OF THE NATIONAL ASSOCIATION OF MUTILATED AND INVALID WAR VETERANS, WHO PRODUCED THEM UNTIL 1949.

The 500 C reached the market in March 1949. The front end was redesigned; the fenders and horizontal slat grille were a single piece, a feature found in the 615 light commercial (1950) and the city bus 401 (1952). Fenders were not incorporated into the body until 1950 in the 1400 sedan, the first Fiat to adopt the "ponton" line. The engine was still a 569 cc, but the head was in aluminum and a heater with vents to defog the windshield was standard equipment. In addition to the sedan, there were the Giardiniera and the van. The former was replaced in 1952 by the Belvedere. It had doors and side panels in pressed sheet metal with pastel color finishes, and dark colored hoods, fenders, roofs, and profiles while the side and door panels were lighter, tone on tone or contrasting depending on the color. At NSU-Fiat, where production resumed in 1951, the Belvedere was produced in solid colors with smooth side panels. Italy was a country under reconstruction, and its need for efficient vehicles guaranteed that the "C" would be more successful than its predecessors. A total of 376,370 were produced by Mirafiori, including sedans (made until 1954) and Belvederes (1955) in addition to the 9,040 produced by NSU-Fiat. In all, Fiat produced 519,646 500 As, Bs and Cs, including the chassis sold to bodyworks.

Because there was no mass-produced sports version in the line, many bodyworks bought Topolinos of all three series and fitted them out with their own bodies. The small series produced included two Zagatos with integrated fenders: the Panoramica, which offered a lot of headroom inside, and the Gran Luce, whose sloping roof defigned its coupé shape. The Italian car-tuning shop and manufacturer Siata operated on two opposite fronts. On one hand, it transformed the 500 into the Amica, a "ponton"-style sports car, and on the other it used the 500 to develop a forward control van, produced during the war and used as a base for ambulances. In 1949, Nash used the mechanical design of the 500 C for its NXI (Nash Experimental International), a prototype designed by Bill Fajole. The small two-seater roadster with a monocoque body was destined for the American market, but it was to be produced outside the U.S. to limit manufacturing costs. Italy was initially the chosen partner, but the currency exchange

rates between the dollar and the pound made it more convenient to manufacture the car in the United Kingdom, using the mechanical design of the Austin to produce the Nash Metropolitan, available as a coupé or a roadster.

However, most of the special-edition 500s were artisanal, constructed by car buffs and "gentleman drivers." Many of them participated in grueling competitions like the Mille Miglia with standard models, but those who hoped to win or place bought a bare frame and had it fitted out as a roadster or barchetta. The phenomenon became particularly important in the postwar period, when competition flourished and frames became readily available from damaged private vehicles or from the Arar, a government agency that sold ex-military vehicles and abandoned vehicles whose owners could not be identified. The cars often had

36-37 ELIO ZAGATO WITH TWO OF THE 500-BASED BARCHETTAS BUILT BY THE COACHBUILDING COMPANY FOUNDED BY HIS FATHER, UGO, IN 1919.

37 A ZAGATO BARCHETTA, PROBABLY THE SAME ONE SEEN ON THE RIGHT IN THE LARGE PHOTO. THE ZAGATOS WERE BUILT ON COMMISSION BY GENTLEMAN DRIVERS, WITH THE EXCEPTION OF THE GRAN LUCE AND THE PANORAMICA, WHICH WERE PRODUCED IN A SMALL SERIES.

standard-equipment engines that had been modified with an increased-flow carburetor or a special exhaust system, but sometimes the frames carried higher-performance engines such as the Lancia Ardea engine or the engine of the Wehrmacht's BMW R75 motorcycle. The first car designed by Nuccio Bertone was a used 500 A, which he transformed into a barchetta racecar. It made his father's bodyworks one of the most famous names in Italian style. Some 500s were transformed into electric cars, particularly in Italy and France, in an era when battery-run vehicles were common for city transportation.

38 ELIO ZAGATO, RACING ONE OF HIS BARCHETTAS WITH THE NAME OF HIS COACHBUILDING COMPANY VERY PROMINENTLY WRITTEN ON THE GRILLE, FOR PUBLICITY. RACECARS WERE TYPICALLY RIGHT-HAND DRIVE UNTIL THE END OF THE 60S.

39 TOP THE SPOTORNO-MOSCATELLI TEAM AT THE 1938 MILLE MIGLIA WITH A 500-BASED SPIDER. THE ENGINE WAS TUNED WITH A SIATA HEAD.

39 BOTTOM A STANDARD 500 C IN WHICH THE ENGINE WAS TUNED WITH A SUPERBA HEAD, IN VIALE VENEZIA IN BRESCIA, WAITING FOR THE START OF THE MILLE MIGLIA IN 1952, WITH THE TEAM OF LUCIANO GIANNI AND MARIO RIBONI ON BOARD.

40 TOP SANDRO FIORIO, FATHER OF THE TEAM MANAGER AND DRIVER, CESARE FIORIO, WITH PIERINO AVALLE IN A 500 WITH A SIATA HEAD, AT THE STARTING LINE OF THE 1948 MILLE MIGLIA. AVALLE AND HIS BROTHER MARIO HAD A TUNING COMPANY IN TURIN.

40 BOTTOM AVALLE AND FIORIO AT THE 1947 MILLE MIGLIA, ABOARD THEIR SIATA 500-BASED BARCHETTA. THEY CAME IN SECOND IN THEIR CATEGORY, WITH A TIME OF 22H29'42".

40-41 FONTANELLA'S 500 BARCHETTA AT THE STARTING LINE OF THE 19TH ITALIAN GRAND PRIX IN VALENTINO PARK IN TURIN ON SEPTEMBER 5, 1948. THE CO-PILOT SEAT IS COVERED WITH A TONNEAU.

OFFICINE PATRIARCA

VIA AVEZZANO, 9 · ROMA · TELEFONO 776.958

LA MONOPOSTO CORSA

PATRIARCA
Fiat 500

42-43 VITO AND VITTORINO BARION IN THE AERODYNAMIC 500 TUROLLA, AN EXAMPLE OF AN UNCOMMON CLOSED-ROOF RACECAR, AT THE STARTING LINE OF THE 1948 MILLE MIGLIA.

43 THE ROMAN AUTO BUILDING AND TUNING COMPANY, PATRIARCA USED THE MECHANICS OF THE TOPOLINO TO MAKE A SMALL SERIES OF ONE-SEATERS WITH OPEN WHEELS, WHICH WAS FOLLOWED BY THE BABY, WITH A 500 TWIN-CYLINDER ENGINE.

44-45 DANTE GIACOSA AT THE END OF THE '60S, BETWEEN A TOPOLINO SEDAN, WHICH WAS JUST BEGINNING TO ATTRACT THE ATTENTION OF COLLECTORS, AND A 500 L, THE MAXIMUM EVOLUTION OF THE "110" PROJECT AT THE TIME.

The birth of a pop icon

Italy did not have to wait long for another 500 after the Topolino. The engineering department of Deutsche Fiat in Heilbronn (created in 1952 and led by Antonio Fessia, who returned to work for Fiat before going to work for Lancia in 1955) designed a city car to satisfy the requests of both the market and the unions. These were times of misery, and Germany was full of two-seater microcars with three or four wheels and two-stroke engines. Italy was faring better, but most of its vehicles were motorcycles, in part because the microcars had failed to catch on.

Giacosa told of projects that were already under way in 1939: "Another project I remember with regret was for a vehicle that was smaller than the 500 (Topolino—Ed.), called the 400. I've always preferred small cars. From the time I was a child, growing up in a family with limited resources, (. . .) I learned that nothing should be wasted (. . .); paying close attention to the financial aspect of a problem when trying to solve it has always been a great help for me."

45 THE "MASCHERONE," AN OLD WOODEN FRAME OF THE "PROJECT 110" 500, WHICH WAS REVISED A NUMBER OF TIMES, IS ON DISPLAY AT THE FIAT HISTORICAL CENTER. THE DIFFERENT COLORS OF WOOD REPRESENT THE VARIOUS FACELIFTS THAT IT UNDERWENT OVER THE YEARS.

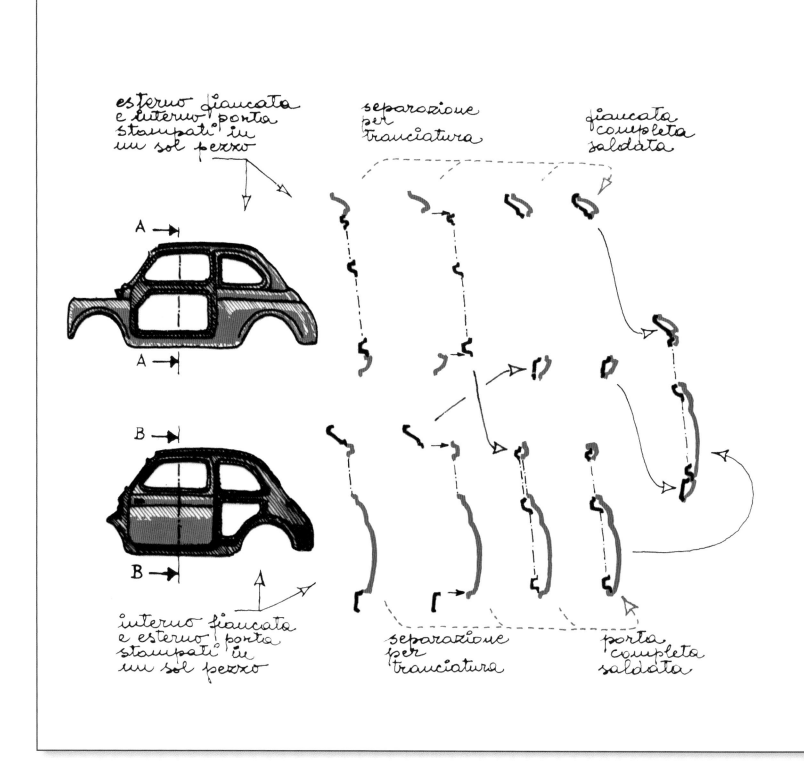

esterno fiancata e interno porta stampati in un sol pezzo

separazione per tranciatura

fiancata completa saldata

A → ←
A → ←

B → ←
B → ←

interno fiancata e esterno porta stampati in un sol pezzo

separazione per tranciatura

porta completa saldata

46   THE DESIGN OF THE SIDES OF THE 500 WAS ONE OF GIACOSA'S MASTERPIECES. THE DESIGNS SEEN ON THESE PAGES ARE ALSO HIS: SHAPES AND SIZES THAT FIT TOGETHER PERFECTLY IN ORDER TO REDUCE WASTE.

47   FROM GIACOSA'S NOTES, THE CONSTRUCTION OF THE SIDES FOR MOLDING, CUTTING, AND WELDING. THE SAME SHEET OF METAL WAS USED TO MAKE THE SIDE PANELS AND THE DOORFRAME (OR, ON THE CONTRARY, FOR THE SIDE FRAME AND THE DOOR PANELS).

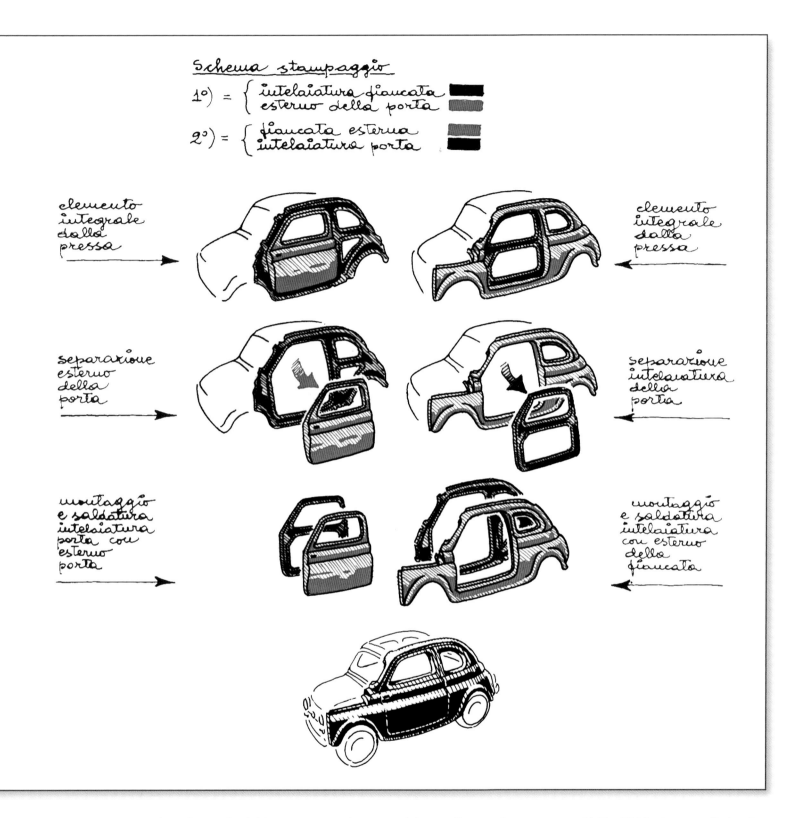

Fessia commissioned two front-wheel-drive prototypes, the F03 and the F05 (for Forschung, or research). The F03 had a two-cylinder air-cooled engine, and the F05 had a water-cooled engine, derived from the four-cylinder engine of the 1100/103. When the F05 was test-driven in Turin, the Pino Torinese road proved fatal for the constant-velocity joints and the front axle. In 1953, Hans-Peter Bauhof, an engineer from the Weinsberg factory, produced a hatchback with an ILO motorcycle engine that strongly resembled the definitive 500, except for the beltline on the front end, which was lower. The Turin factory found the body very interesting and put Giacosa in charge of developing it. It had to be a real automobile with a very low price that would emancipate the middle class, attract motorcycle and scooter riders, and introduce women to the world of cars. It had to have at least 13 HP, reach speeds of 53 miles per hour (85 kph), and consume no more than 1.2 gallons (4.5 l) per 62 miles (100 km). It had to be built with as little sheet metal as possible, and it had to be under 10.8 feet (3.3 m) long.

48-49 QUALITY CONTROL AND APPROVAL OF THE NUOVA 500 AT THE END OF THE ASSEMBLY LINE IN THE MIRAFIORI FACTORY IN TURIN. THE NEARBY LINES PRODUCED THE 600, THE 1100/103, AND THE 1400/1900.

49 PRESENTATION OF THE NUOVA 500 AT A FIAT DEALERSHIP. THE STORK WAS PROBABLY THE WORK OF AEROSTUDIO BORGHI, WHO HAD PROPOSED A SIMILAR ONE TO LANCIA.

Giacosa wanted a vertical-twin-cylinder air-cooled engine, made with an aluminum crankcase and separate cast-iron pipes, a camshaft in the crankcase with rods and rocker arms and intake manifolds produced when the head was cast. A rear, longitudinal 479 cc engine was suspended on the chassis with a pantograph to absorb vibrations, cooled by a fan, coaxial with the dynamo, which circulated air inside the fairing that encapsulated it. An issue of space made it necessary to develop a centrifugal oil filter, which turned out to be so efficient that it was also used in many other Fiats. The differential and the non-synchronous four-speed transmission with synchromesh, which required double-clutching during the downshift, were one block. The engine was designed by Giovanni Torazza, the transmission by Angelo Mosso. The independent front axle had telescopic shock absorbers and transverse leaf springs, while the rear axle had swing-arm suspension and coil springs. The car had hydraulic drum brakes.

In 1954, the director of the automotive design department, Giuseppe Alberti, prepared a model that utilized many of the 600's car body parts and one inspired by Bauhof's prototype, with the front end a little bit higher on the beltline. The second model was chosen; it was an essential, no-frills product, typical of Italian industrial design. So that it would not become competition for the 600, the sales and marketing director decided to make it a 2+2, with two front seats and two makeshift seats in the back, and decreased the engine size by a couple of HP. Both were errors that would be corrected during the vehicle's first years on the market.

FROM CREATION TO LEGEND: NUOVA 500 (1957-1960)

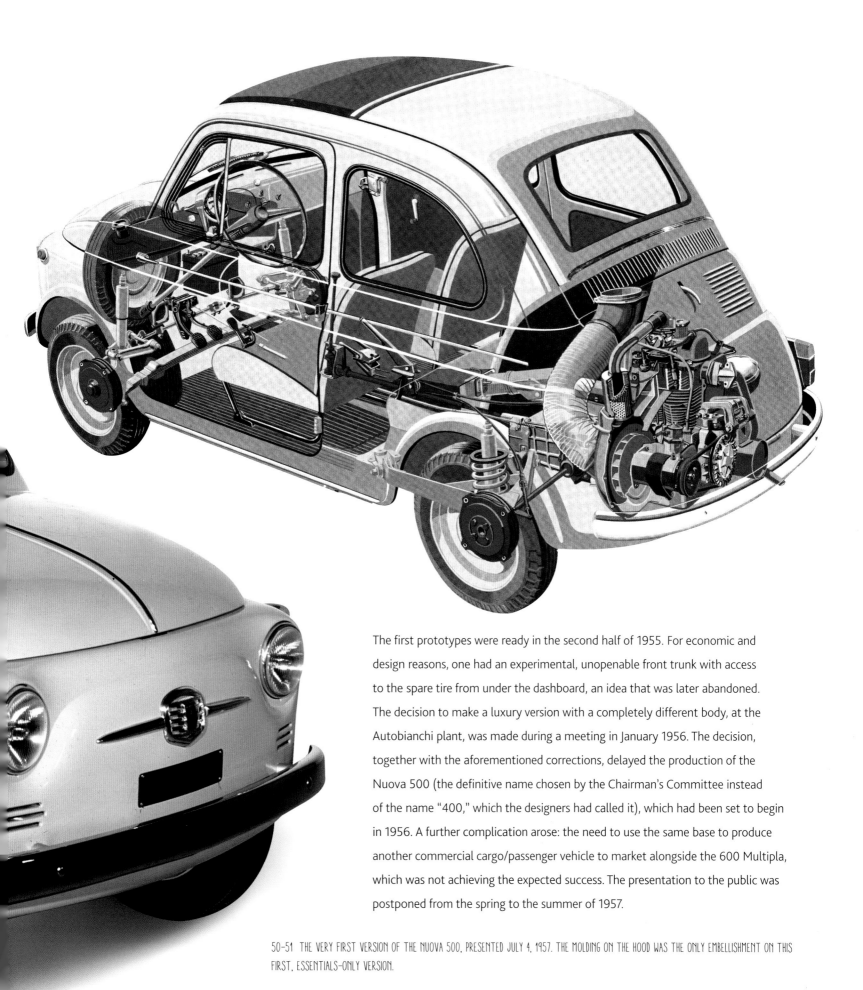

The first prototypes were ready in the second half of 1955. For economic and design reasons, one had an experimental, unopenable front trunk with access to the spare tire from under the dashboard, an idea that was later abandoned. The decision to make a luxury version with a completely different body, at the Autobianchi plant, was made during a meeting in January 1956. The decision, together with the aforementioned corrections, delayed the production of the Nuova 500 (the definitive name chosen by the Chairman's Committee instead of the name "400," which the designers had called it), which had been set to begin in 1956. A further complication arose: the need to use the same base to produce another commercial cargo/passenger vehicle to market alongside the 600 Multipla, which was not achieving the expected success. The presentation to the public was postponed from the spring to the summer of 1957.

50-51 THE VERY FIRST VERSION OF THE NUOVA 500, PRESENTED JULY 4, 1957. THE MOLDING ON THE HOOD WAS THE ONLY EMBELLISHMENT ON THIS FIRST, ESSENTIALS-ONLY VERSION.

51 A CUTAWAY DRAWING OF THE NUOVA 500. THIS VERSION, THE TETTO APRIBILE (SUNROOF), WAS INTRODUCED IN MARCH 1959 AND SOLD ALONGSIDE THE TRASFORMABILE, WHOSE CONVERTIBLE CLOTH TOP OPENED ALL THE WAY TO THE BACK GRILLE.

52 THE NUOVA 500 TRASFORMABILE SEEN FROM ABOVE IN AN IMAGE THAT WAS SUPPOSED TO HIGHLIGHT ITS SIZE, SUITABLE FOR A FAMILY OF THREE; TODAY, THAT IMAGE HIGHLIGHTS ITS LIMITS.

52-53 A BODY FITTED OUT AND CUT TO TAKE PICTURES FOR THE CATALOG. CHILDREN ARE SITTING ON A MAT PLACED ON THE BACK BENCH, WHICH HAD NO PADDING.

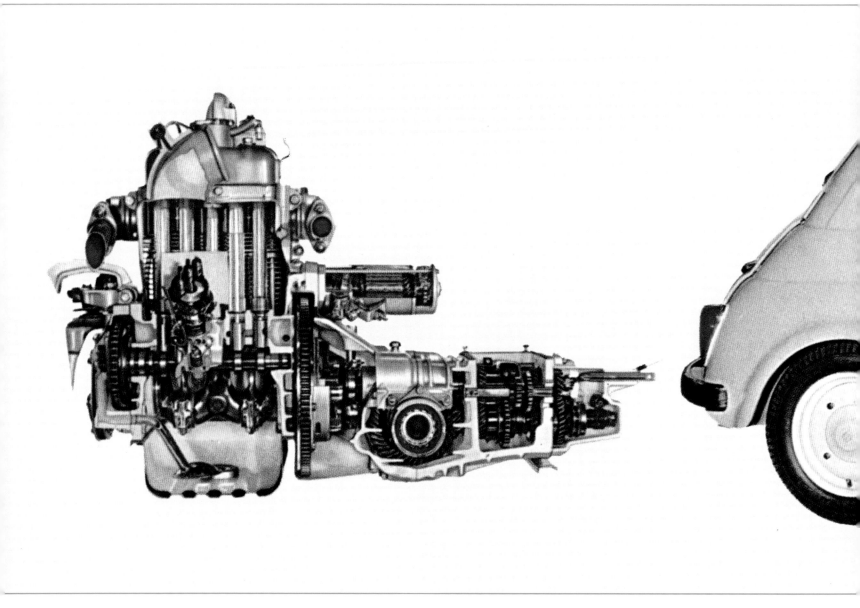

The launch of the Nuova 500 was a well-prepared media event. On July 1, 1957, Professor Valletta was at the Viminale, the seat of the Prime Minister, where the premier, Adone Zoli, tried the new car, driven by Carlo Salamano, the lead test driver and ex-racecar driver, the same man who had rejected the F05 project after the climb up the Pino Torinese road. Following the presentation, twenty 500s were donated to the Ministry of Labor. On the following Tuesday, the Nuova 500 was revealed to the press at the Sporting Circle of Turin, the summer headquarters of the Press Circle, and on Wednesday the city was flooded with a swarm of 500s that departed from the dealership in Corso Bramante, past the Mirafiori plant, through Piazza San Carlo and Via Roma to arrive in Piazza Castello. The press and the new postwar television followed the caravan. The cars were carrying the candidates that would participate in the Miss Italy finals in September, which aroused a lot of interest. The press release read "Twenty years after the original 500, the Nuova 500 is riding a wave of equal success; completely new and modern, lower-priced, more economical, a worthy successor to the world's first economy car, produced by the Turin-based Fiat." The service cars that were following the caravan provided the opportunity, perhaps involuntarily, to make a comparison. The camera operators were driving 500 Cs and the police were aboard Gilera Saturno motorcycles, which both had the same size engine and price as the new economy car.

54-55 ON THE LEFT, A LONGITUDINAL SECTION OF THE ENGINE AND TRANSMISSION; `ON THE RIGHT, ANOTHER VIEW OF THE CUT CHASSIS. WITH NO PASSENGERS, THE LACK OF PADDING IN THE FRONT SEATS CAN BE SEEN.

55 THE HORIZONTAL VERSION OF THE 500 ENGINE, INTRODUCED IN 1960 FOR THE GIARDINIERA, MADE IT POSSIBLE TO KEEP THE CARGO COMPARTMENT LOW AND EASILY ACCESSIBLE.

56 IN THIS ADVERTISING ILLUSTRATION FOR THE LAUNCH OF THE NUOVA 500, THE CAR IS SURROUNDED BY THE PUBLIC AND CAMERAMEN TO HIGHLIGHT HOW IMPORTANT THE NEWS OF THE LAUNCH WAS.

57 A STUDIO SHOT OF THE NUOVA 500 NORMALE LAUNCHED IN THE AUTUMN OF 1957. ITS HUBCAPS AND ALUMINUM MOLDINGS ON THE SIDES AND DOORSILLS WERE IDENTIFYING FEATURES.

As a film review would say, the Nuova 500 earned critical acclaim but was not a success with the public. Its balanced lines were much more pleasant and fun than those of the 600. Engineers and designers applauded the intelligent industrial solutions, such as using the same sheet of metal for the side panels and the doorframe that won it the 1959 Golden Compass Award. The 500 cost 490,000 ITL as opposed to 640,000 ITL for the 600 and one million ITL for the 1100/103. An installment plan was available through Sava, the finance company created by Fiat in 1929 to sell the 509 on installments. Sava is now part of FCA Bank.

The date of the launch was close to the summer vacation period, a moment in which Italian families already had extra expenses. In addition, the price of the 500 was almost the same as that of the bigger and better-performing 600, despite its stark equipment. These two factors combined to hold back sales. The car's overly essential trim was initially blamed and, in fact, in some cases it was really too austere. The side windows were unopenable and there was no device to secure the deflectors in an intermediate position. The back seat was a simple sheet of metal covered in imitation leather, more useful for luggage than for two children or as a makeshift seat for two adults. The dashboard was also essential with a clearly readable instrument panel that had indicator lights for the car lights, the dynamo, the odometer, and the fuel level. The unmovable seat backs were covered with checked cloth (imitation leather was available on demand) that left the metal structure visible on the sides. The ignition key at the center of the dashboard commanded the lights, and two levers located on the transmission tunnel between the seats commanded the starter motor and the choke. The heater, which was an optional feature, drew hot air in from the engine compartment through the central tunnel. Ventilation was also dynamic: air came in through the grille under the headlights and through the tunnels to reach the passenger compartment. The fuel tank and the spare tire were under the front hood, behind the front panel. There was room for a toolbox and one thin suitcase.

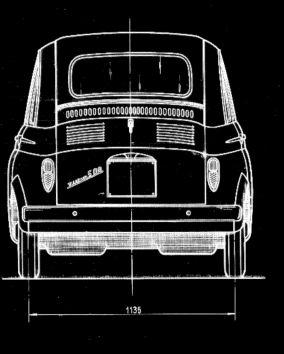

1135

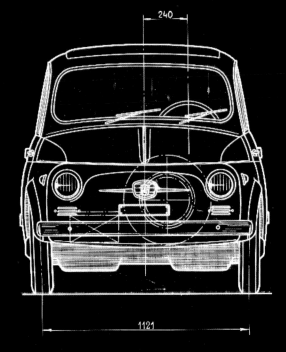

240

1121

715

1115~

915~

850~

960~

340~ (290÷415)

540~ (590÷465)

218~

630

340~

418~

488~

230~

300~

Entrata 1184~

1116~

1298~

125~

182~

125-12"   512x120

65   430~   P.1840   580~   55

2850~

2970~

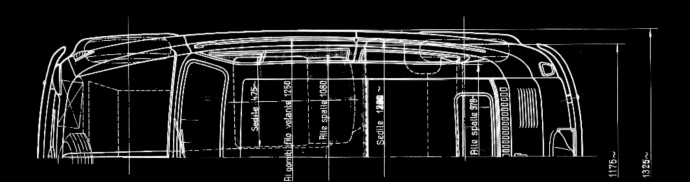

Sedile 475~

Al gomiti filo volante 1250

Alle spalle 1080

Sedile 1220~

Alle spalle 978~

1175~

1325~

In October 1957, a larger carburetor jet increased the power of the engine to 15 HP, the same as the prototypes. It was the first correction made to the conditions imposed by the shortsighted sales and marketing office, and it led from what buffs today call the pre-N series to the series that became known as the "N" series. It was available in two versions: the Nuova 500 Economica had the same features as the model presented in July, while the Normale had aluminum moldings along the beltline and on the doorsill, aluminum-framed windows that rolled down, aluminum hubcaps, and the Nuova 500 emblem on the hood. The commutator key was replaced by a light switch; the turn signals were controlled with two levers on the steering column; the bench got a bit of padding; and the sides of the seat backs were covered. The Normale cost the same as the first version, 490,000 ITL, and the Economica cost 465,000 ITL. Those who had purchased the old model received a check for 25,000 ITL from Fiat.

The version destined for the American market came out at the end of the year. It was characterized by large, cone-shaped bumper guards and externally mounted headlights (initially English, supplied by Lucas Industries, and then Italian, a few months after production began) that were placed higher than usual, giving the 500 the look of an affable frog.

58 SIDE AND PLAN VIEWS OF THE FIRST VERSION OF THE 500 TETTO APRIBILE, WHICH HAD THE EMBELLISHMENTS OF THE NORMALE BUT DID NOT YET CONFORM TO THE 1959 HIGHWAY CODE.

59 A NUOVA 500 TETTO APRIBILE IN A VERSION THAT WAS PRODUCED FOR A FEW MONTHS IN 1959. IT STILL HAD ITS INDICATOR LIGHTS ON THE FENDERS AND AIR INTAKE VENTS UNDER THE HEADLIGHTS.

In March 1958, the heating system was extended to the front area and even though heaters were still optional, they were mounted in almost the entire production run. In September, a higher compression ratio increased power to 16.5 HP. But despite the improvements and the reduction in prices, 390,000 ITL for the Economica and 430,000 ITL for the Normale, sales declined. Another serious error imposed by the sales and marketing department was corrected at the Mirafiori plant and led to the creation of a new version with a semi-convertible top that opened only above the front seat. The roof was higher than the completely convertible version, making the car's interior more comfortable. The new version, called Tetto apribile (sunroof), was displayed at the Geneva Car Show in 1959, alongside the convertible version whose name had been changed to Economica Trasformabile (convertible). Both versions finally had a padded back seat that officially made them four-seaters. The market showed that the 500 and 600 were not competitors. The new series had light-colored imitation leather semicircles on the backrests in the back seat; they were to become one of the 500's characterizing features for the next ten years. The versions of the Trasformabile (the word "Economica" had been dropped from the name) and the Tetto apribile, which had been updated to conform with the 1959 Highway Code, appeared very soon afterwards. They no longer had turn signals on the fenders, and the vents under the front headlights were replaced with bezels that encased double-filament bulbs that served as parking lights and turn signals. This modification makes it easy to confuse these models with the later 500 Ds. The taillights were bigger and had a turn signal that was orange rather than red.

60 ADVERTISEMENT FOR THE 500 TRASFORMABILE AND TETTO APRIBILE, UPDATED TO CONFORM WITH THE NEW HIGHWAY CODE. THE AIR INTAKE VENTS WERE REPLACED WITH INDICATOR LIGHTS THAT ALSO SERVED AS POSITION LIGHTS.

61 ONE OF THE LAST "OLD CODE" NUOVA 500 TRASFORMABILES, IN AN ELEGANT DARK GRAY THAT ENHANCED THE CHROME DETAILS ADDED DURING THE VARIOUS FACELIFTS THAT IT UNDERWENT DURING ITS FIRST TWO YEARS OF PRODUCTION.

The American models, all of which were now sunroofs, were also modified. The vents under the headlights remained, and the turn signals/parking lights were mounted higher. The big logo on the back of the new version created for the German market, the Luxus, made it easily recognizable.

From July 1957 to October 1960, when Mirafiori was probably the biggest and most modern automobile factory in the world, it produced 181,000 pre-Ns and Ns. About 120,000 were produced in the last two years, a sign of the appreciation that finally began to spread among the population, from the cultural elite to the general public, which would never again abandon the Nuova 500. A pop icon was born, a "cheap and chic" auto that would be an ambassador of Italy's lifestyle and design. Many 500s turned out to be the only car that many families had, but it was with the 500 that the phenomenon of a second family car began. The Turin plant followed the entire production cycle and, unlike what had happened with the 600s or the 1100s, it produced the 500s for all the markets in the world.

62 TO HIGHLIGHT ITS "ITALIAN STYLE," THIS ILLUSTRATION OF THE 500 AMERICA IS SET IN FLORENCE, EVEN THOUGH THE CAR WAS NOT FOR SALE IN ITALY.

62-63 ANOTHER AMERICAN MODEL, THIS TIME IN A QUINTESSENTIAL AMERICAN SETTING, A FAR WEST GENERAL STORE, A MINER WITH HIS MULE AND A PIN-UP GIRL AT THE WHEEL.

64 A CLOSED-ROOF 500 SPORT AT THE HOCKENHEIM 12 HOURS.

64-65 THE POST-1959 500 SPORT WITH INDICATOR LIGHTS UNDER THE HEADLIGHTS. THE SPORT NEVER HAD MOLDINGS ON THE BELTLINE.

THE COMPACT RACECAR: NUOVA 500 SPORT (1957–1960)

The Mirafiori plant also produced the Sport version, with a 110.04 engine bored out to 499.5 cc—the maximum size allowed to race in the Turismo 500 cc category—that delivered 21 HP at 4,600 rpm. Production of an extremely limited series began in 1958. Carlo Abarth helped to develop the model, but he did not affix his signature scorpion to the 500. Mechanical preparation included increased engine displacement, obtained by re-boring the cylinder lines by 1.4 mm, increased compression ratio of 8.6:1, larger valves, profiled pistons, redesigned combustion chambers, a Weber inverted carburetor, larger springs and valves, a polished intake manifold, and a larger fan. Its maximum speed was 65 miles per hour (105 kph). The Sport, available only in white, was a Normale without the chrome profiles on the beltline, with a red stripe painted down the side. It was the only 500 to leave the Fiat factory with a completely closed roof. The version with a sunroof, introduced in 1959, cost 495,000 ITL, and the closed-roof version that was immediately available cost 560,000 ITL. Before it was officially put on the market, it arrived in first place at both the Hockenheim 12 hours and the Liege-Brescia-Liege. The last Nuova 500 Sports were made using the body of the 500 D.

THE PROOF: 500 D (1960–1964)

In October 1960, the 110D.000 engine was mounted on the chassis of the 1959 model, which had been updated to conform with the new Highway Code. Engine displacement was the same as that of the Sport. Horsepower was decreased to 17.5 HP for the normal versions, and a number of details were revised to increase reliability. This was the birth of the 500 D, which was also used to produce the Sport version (with the same mechanics), the American version, and the German Luxus. The backseat was a small padded sofa with a fold-down backrest that became a luggage stand. No other improvements were made; everyone liked the 500, and it no longer needed corrections. The 1961 model had padded sun visors, a manual windshield washer pump, and an ashtray in the middle of the dashboard. In 1964, one year before the 500 D went out of production, the door moldings were shortened, moving them farther from the door handle. A total of 640,000 500 Ds was produced.

66 THE 500 D VERSION OF THE BAMBINA, AS THE 500 WAS CALLED IN NEW ZEALAND FROM 1959 TO 1969. IT WAS ASSEMBLED AT TORINO MOTORS WITH ITALIAN COMPONENTS AND WAS EVEN USED IN THE ANTARCTIC.

66-67 FROM THE OUTSIDE, THE 500 D INTRODUCED AT THE END OF 1960 WAS THE SAME AS THE LAST NUOVA 500. THE DIFFERENCE WAS IN THE INTERIOR: THE NEW VERSION HAD A PADDED BACK SEAT.

ONE MILLION CITY CARS: 500 F (1965-1972)

The 1965 500 F introduced a reinforced clutch, differential, and axle shaft. The Highway Code had begun to prohibit the so-called "suicide"—or rear-hinged—doors that were considered a possible cause of accidents. The new doors opened against the wind, and the hinges were recessed. The F abandoned the bolted roof of the Sunroof version in favor of one molded with the pillars, with a curvature that further improved interior comfort. The only metal body parts that remained the same as the D were the hood and the rear transom; everything else was redesigned, albeit imperceptibly.

The molding halfway up the side was eliminated, but the one on the doorsill remained. The engine (type 110F.000) had reinforced exhaust manifold connections, valves with double return springs, and a PCV valve in the tappet lid, which was made of pressed—no longer cast—metal. In the first ten months of production, four bolts per side were used to fix the recessed hinges to the body, rather than the two bolts that would be used in later models—and in fact, the models produced in 1965–1966 (vehicle identification numbers up to one million, approximately) are fondly called "eight bolts" by buffs.

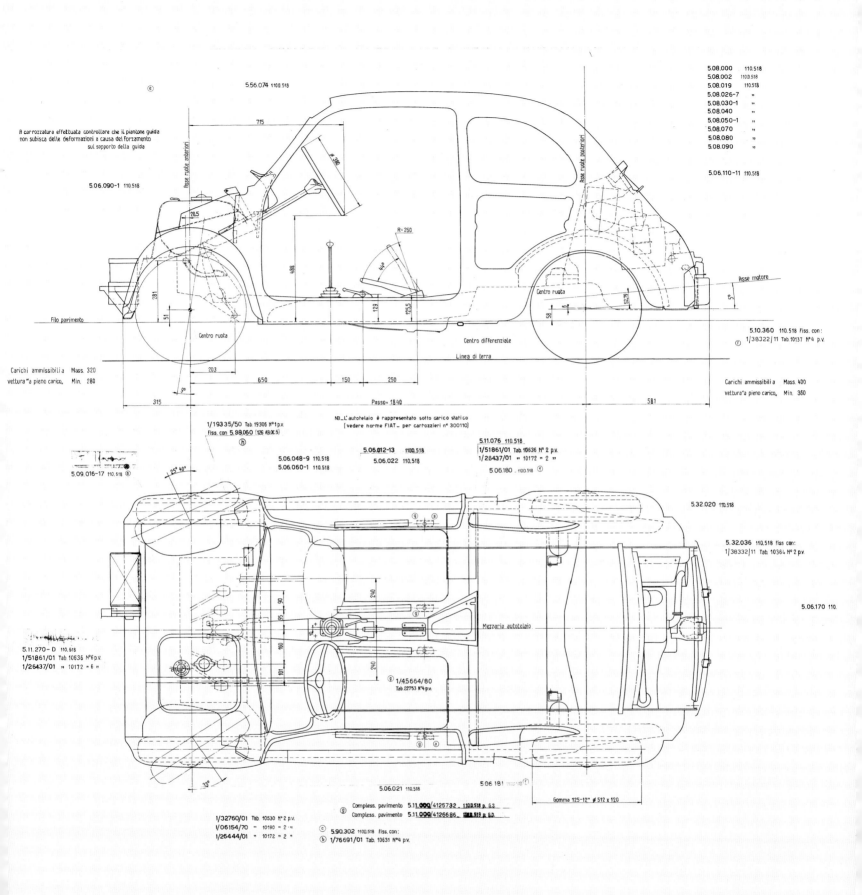

69 SIDE AND PLAN VIEWS OF THE MONOCOQUE BODY OF THE 500 D, WITHOUT ITS WINDOWS, EXTERNAL MOVING PARTS SUCH AS DOORS AND HOODS,
A FRONT END, OR FRONT BUMPERS.

ONE MILLION CITY CARS: 500 F (1965–1972)

The 1965 500 F introduced a reinforced clutch, differential, and axle shaft. The Highway Code had begun to prohibit the so-called "suicide"—or rear-hinged—doors that were considered a possible cause of accidents. The new doors opened against the wind, and the hinges were recessed. The F abandoned the bolted roof of the Sunroof version in favor of one molded with the pillars, with a curvature that further improved interior comfort. The only metal body parts that remained the same as the D were the hood and the rear transom; everything else was redesigned, albeit imperceptibly.

The molding halfway up the side was eliminated, but the one on the doorsill remained. The engine (type 110F.000) had reinforced exhaust manifold connections, valves with double return springs, and a PCV valve in the tappet lid, which was made of pressed—no longer cast—metal. In the first ten months of production, four bolts per side were used to fix the recessed hinges to the body, rather than the two bolts that would be used in later models—and in fact, the models produced in 1965–1966 (vehicle identification numbers up to one million, approximately) are fondly called "eight bolts" by buffs.

70-71 SIDE VIEW OF THE 500 F. ALTHOUGH ALMOST ALL
ITS BODY PANELS WERE REDESIGNED, THE ONLY OBVIOUS
DIFFERENCE FROM THE D WAS THE CURVE OF ITS ROOF.

71 A CUTAWAY DRAWING OF THE MECHANICS OF THE 500 F. IN
1966, WITH THE F, PRODUCTION RUN OF THE 500 "TIPO 110"
REACHED ONE MILLION UNITS.

72 THE FRONT BADGE ON THE FIRST VERSION OF THE 500 F
STILL HAD A SMALL GRILLE AND MOUSTACHE WINGS.

73 IN 1968, THE 500 F BEGAN MOUNTING A DIAMOND-SHAPED
BADGE LIKE THAT OF THE L AND THE R ON THE HOOD.

In March 1966, the eight screws that held the back grille in place were reduced to three. The headlight and taillight bezels were no longer in aluminum, a material that the F would gradually abandon over the long years of its career. During the first months of production, the material used to make the door handles was switched to steel; and beginning in 1966, plastic was used to make headlight, taillight, and license-plate bezels as well as the anterior grille, which had become a single piece with the emblem wings. Beginning in 1967, hubcaps were produced in steel; and in 1968, the model underwent a purely esthetic restyling that rendered some of its components the same as those of the new 500 L. The front emblem became smaller, the same as that of the 124, so the header panel had to be modified; the diamond-shaped back emblem read "Fiat 500" instead of "Nuova 500," identical to the 1957 emblem and, at that point, rather senseless; and the seats were solid-colored, without the lighter-colored crescent. The last update, made in 1970, moved the license plate light a little higher and introduced the steering wheel lock.

74-75 THE 1969 500 L WAS BUILT ON THE BASE OF THE 500 F, BUT ITS EXTERIOR AND INTERIOR DETAILS WERE MORE LUXURIOUS. THE TUBULAR BUMPER PROTECTORS WERE A DISTINGUISHING FEATURE OF ITS EXTERIOR.

75 THE INTERIOR OF THE 500 L HAD VERTICALLY QUILTED SEATS, A HORIZONTAL RECTANGULAR SPEEDOMETER INSPIRED BY THE ONE IN THE 850 SPECIAL, AND A BLACK PLASTIC DASHBOARD.

CITY CAR LUXURY: 500 L (1968–1972)

In August 1968, two trim packages were available. The updated 500 F was still the basic version, while the luxury version, the L, had tubular bumper protectors, more padding in the vertically quilted seats, a simple rectangular speedometer like the one in the 850 Special, a black steering wheel with fretwork, carpet, radial tires, chrome accessories, and new hubcaps. The diamond-shaped emblem in the back said "500 L." The new colors that were available included some that would always be iconic, such as Positano Yellow and Night Blue. It was a period of strong social tensions, and each of these colors took on a political significance: the first was for progressives, the second for conservatives. Mechanically speaking, the L was nothing other than an F, which is why the two had the same vehicle identification numbers. Until 1971, all 500s were produced at the Mirafiori plant; then the lines were moved to the Autobianchi plant in Desio (where both the Bianchina Sedan and the Primula had gone out of production) and to the new Sicilfiat plant in Termini Imerese in the province of Palermo. By 1972, 2,443,000 500 Fs and Ls had been produced, including approximately 90,000 at the Autobianchi plant and 80,000 at Sicilfiat.

Gioco della Fiat 500 L

Della 500 L c'è anche una versione ragazzi.
Una versione che ciascuno si può costruire.
I pezzi sono su questa pagina.
Seguendo le istruzioni, il montaggio sarà molto semplice.
Buon divertimento e buon viaggio con la «500 L ragazzi».

Staccare la doppia
pagina ed incollarla
su un cartone leggero.

Ritagliare lungo
la linea continua.
Le linee tratteggiate
servono per le piegature.

Ritagliare lungo le linee continue
nell'ordine:
A pianale-fiancata-cruscotto;
B sedile posteriore;
C sedile anteriore destro;
D sedile anteriore sinistro;

Le superfici colorate in
grigio servono da giunture,
usando la colla.

Costruire per primo il
pianale-fiancata-cruscotto.

Costruire poi i sedili anteriori
e posteriori. Sistemare i sedili.
Costruire il volante con il piantone
inserendo quest'ultimo nel
cruscotto e la leva di cambio nel
pianale dopo avervi praticato due
piccole aperture.

Ora ritagliare gli altri particolari:
E scocca o carrozzeria;
F volante con piantone;
G leva cambio e cassettino
   sul tunnel
H tetto apribile
I paraurti anteriore
L paraurti posteriore
M tasche laterali con una mappa

Collegare il tetto apribile a fisarmo-
nica alla carrozzeria.

Fissare le tasche laterali con la
mappa ai lati interni delle porte.
Sistemare i paraurti.
Piegare la carrozzeria e sistemarla.
La 500 è fatta.

qui montare
il sedile
posteriore
B

qui montare
il sedile
anteriore
D

montare G

qui montare
il sedile
anteriore
C

A

✂ Ritagliare lungo la linea continua

– – – Le linee tratteggiate servono per le
piegature.

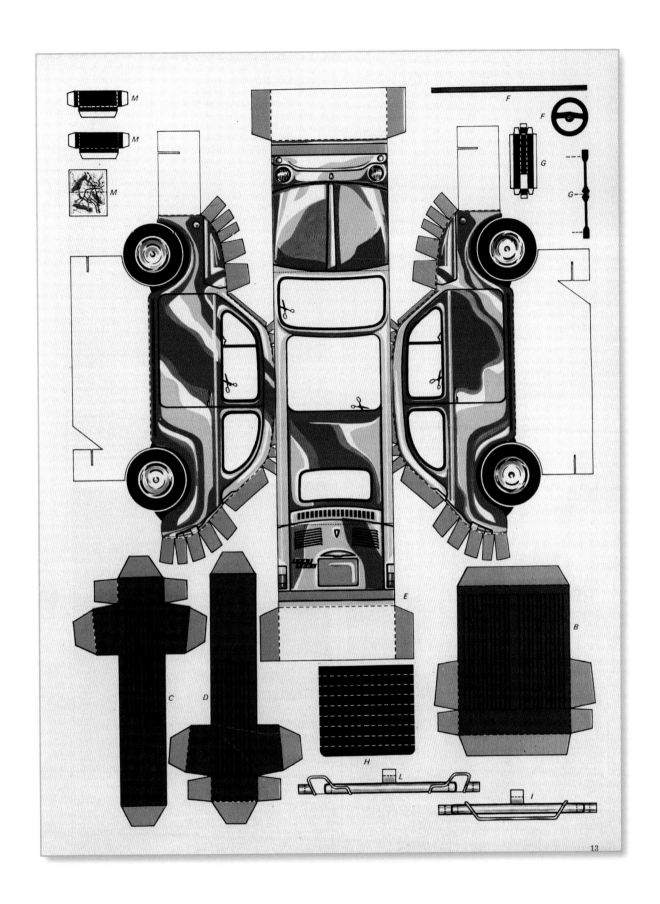

76 AND 77 FROM THE TIME OF THE BALILLA, PARTICULARLY IN THE POSTWAR PERIOD, THE COMPANIES IN THE FIAT GROUP TOOK VERY GOOD CARE OF THEIR YOUNG FANS, WITH MASS-PRODUCED INEXPENSIVE GADGETS. THIS PAPER CAR DEDICATED TO THE 500 L WAS PUBLISHED IN A WEEKLY NEWSPAPER. SINCE THE PAPER WAS LIGHT, THE INSTRUCTIONS ADVISED THE USER TO REINFORCE IT BY TO CUTTING IT OUT AND GLUING IT TO A PIECE OF CARDBOARD.

BACK TO SIMPLICITY: 500 R (1972–1975)

In 1972, after Giacosa had attempted numerous times to improve the 500's comfort while keeping the same lines, the 126 was presented at the Turin Auto Show. The 500 had not yet become the icon that it is today, but it met with remarkable success, a reflection on the need for understatement at the time. Only one version stayed in production; it was simple like the 1957 model. It was called the 500 R (Renewed), and it was, once again, based on the F, with a new front end, molded to accommodate the diamond-shaped logo, and without the moldings on the doorsills. The wheels were the same new, very modern design as those of the 126. The seats were covered in smooth black imitation leather, and the backrest in the backseat was immobile. The engine was the same as that of the 126 (126 A5.000, 594 cc) with horsepower reduced to 18. With a list price that was too close to that of its more modern heir, the 500 R met with modest success, worsened by the 1974 Yom Kippur oil crisis. It stayed in production until 1975, with 34,000 manufactured at the Autobianchi plant (until 1973) and 135,000 at Sicilfiat. On August 1, 1975, a turquoise 500 R rolled off the line, the last to be produced, thus marking the end of the long, exciting career of the most famous Italian car in the world.

THE LITTLE BRATS: 500, 595, AND 695 ABARTH (1957–1972)

The performance of the first 500s was limited, but another 500 existed that performed better; it was produced by the Austrian automaker, Steyr-Puch Werke, with a Fiat body and the company's own mechanics. The first had a 500 cc engine and delivered 16 HP, and those that followed had 650 cc engines that reached 27 and 41 HP. These did not make it to Italy because of another Austrian, Karl Abarth, who became a naturalized Italian with the name Carlo. He was a motorcycle driver, builder, and marketing expert who worked with Pietro Dusio of Cisitalia and Ferdinand Porsche. At the Turin Auto Show in 1957, he presented the "500 Abarth Fiat derivation," a limited series that would be distributed by the network of Fiat dealerships. Its original motor delivered 19 HP and took it to a speed of 62 mph (100 kph). From February 13 to 20, with no advance notice to the press or to Fiat, Abarth had one of his 500s travel around the Monza racetrack speed ring, non-stop. The 500 proved to be safe and reliable, stopping only to refuel and to change drivers. During the trial, about a dozen Fiat executives showed up. The 500 pulverized six of its category's records, averaging a speed of 67.68 mph (108.936 kph) in four days, 67.23 mph (108.200 kph) in five, 67.01 mph (107.850 mph) in six, 67,26 mph (108.252 mph) in seven, 66.92 mph (107.699 kph) over 15,000 km, and 67.04 mph (107.894 kph) over 10,000 miles. Vittorio Valletta summoned Abarth. They drafted a contract for the supply of semi-complete cars and a racing contract that awarded a prize to every Fiat-Abarth that won a race. In 1958, a Pininfarina torpedo body with an Abarth 500 engine broke 28 records in Monza, and all of the 500s that participated in the exhausting Liege-Brescia-Liege placed at the top.

80-81 THE 500 FITTED OUT BY CARLO ABARTH—WITHOUT FIAT'S OFFICIAL SUPPORT—BROKE SIX WORLD RECORDS AT THE MONZA RACETRACK.

81 THE THREE RECORD-WINNING FIAT-ABARTH ONE-SEATERS HAD PININFARINA BODIES. IN FRONT ARE THE 1000 FROM 1960 AND THE 500 FROM 1958, AND IN BACK IS THE 750 FROM 1958.

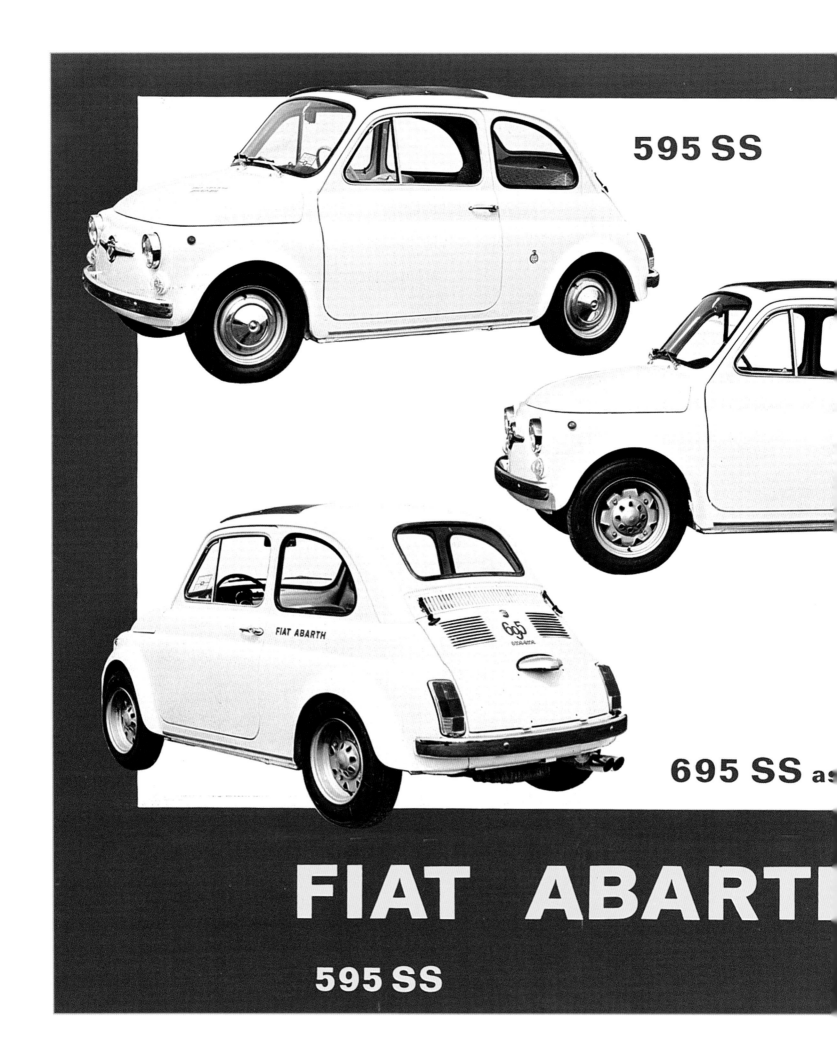

595 SS

695 SS as

FIAT ABARTI

595 SS

695 SS

to corsa

Beginning in mid-1958, the 500 Abarth made room for the 500 Sport and, for a few years, Abarth chased victories and records in larger engine categories and sold 500s, with their original engine displacement, that were aggressive but looked nothing like the standard model.

In 1963, in the era of the 500 D, when production of the Sport had already stopped, he introduced the 595, with displacement increased to 593.7 cc (27 HP at 5,000 rpm, 74 mph). It was based on the 500 D until 1965, then on the first and second series F from '65 to '71. In 1964, two super-sporting versions were added: the 595 SS (32 HP, 86 mph) and the 695 with a 689 cc engine that could reach a maximum speed of 80 mph (130 kph), also available as 695 SS with 38 HP that reached 87 mph (140 kph). Even more aggressive versions dedicated to the racetrack were the 1965 695 SS Assetto Corsa, with a widened wheel track, and the 595 and 695 Competizione, with 50 and 60 HP respectively, capable of reaching up to 105 mph (170 kph). The 500, 595, and 695 Abarth were sold by a network of dealerships separate from that of Fiat. Their look became fiercer over the years, and the versions with bigger engines often had spacers that kept the hood open to improve cooling and, therefore, engine performance. Circulating alongside the models that Abarth created using complete or semi-complete cars were a great number of vehicles that artisanal tuners had "Abarth-ized," installing components or complete Abarth kits in standard models. All his derivatives of the 500 went out of production in 1971, when Carlo Abarth sold his company to Fiat. After that, two more Abarth models were derived from standard models: the Autobianchi A112 and the Ritmo (Strada) 125 TC and 130 TC. When the 595 and 695 went out of production, the private racecar drivers who had been faithful to the 500 turned to Giannini, Abarth's eternal rival, who had begun proposing his tuned 500s in the era of the first Ds.

82-83 THE 595/695 SS RANGE FROM THE MIDDLE OF THE 1960S WAS BASED ON THE 500 F. BASIC VERSIONS WERE IDENTIFIABLE ONLY BY THEIR WHEELS, THEIR EMBLEM, AND THEIR EXHAUST SYSTEM.

83 A 695 BASED ON A 500 D, WITH MAGNESIUM WHEELS BY CAMPAGNOLO. THE BASIC VERSION OF THIS MODEL WAS ALSO ESTHETICALLY VERY DISCREET.

bianchina

LA PICCOLA VETTURA DI GRANDE CLASSE

84-85 A SIDE VIEW OF THE BIANCHINA TRASFORMABILE IN ITS FIRST MONTHS OF PRODUCTION. THE ROSTRUMS THAT REACH THE HEADLIGHTS WERE A RECURRING THEME IN FABIO LUIGI RAPI'S STYLE. IN THE FIRST TWO SERIES AND IN THE BASIC VERSION OF THE THIRD SERIES, THEY COMPLETED THE BUMPER, WHICH DID NOT WRAP AROUND THE EDGE OF THE BODY AS IT DID IN THE 1960 THIRD SERIES SPECIAL D.

MILANESE HAUTE COUTURE: BIANCHINA TRASFORMABILE, BERLINA, AND CABRIOLET (1957–1969)

In the mid-1950s, Fiat was already planning a luxury version of the 500 that would be built by Autobianchi, a joint venture company formed by Bianchi, Fiat, and Pirelli in 1955. It was part of the 110 project and was launched with the name Bianchina on September 16, 1957, at the Museum of Science and Technology in Milan, where a famous photo was taken of the Trasformabile (convertible) with Gianni Agnelli at the wheel and the executives Vittorio Valletta, Giovanni Bianchi, and Alberto Pirelli sitting on the platform beside the car. In its first few years, marketing for the Bianchina took advantage of Bianchi's fame as a builder of luxury cars and victorious bicycles, as well as his Milanese—and therefore fashionable—origins. The improved finishes also helped its success and, in fact, in its first years of production, more Bianchinas were sold than 500s, despite the model's slightly higher price (565,000 ITL). The first Bianchina was a small sedan designed by Fabio Luigi Rapi, a Tuscan designer who had designed the 500 C for Zagato and had created for Fiat's special body department the 8V, the turbine-powered prototype, and the 1100/103 Spider. The Bianchina has one of that creation's distinguishing characteristics, the bumper guards under the headlights and taillights. Just as with the 500, the Bianchina was available only in the Trasformabile version, with fixed B-pillars and a partial roof made of fabric. Its wheelbase was identical to that of the 500 and its dimensions were only slightly different: it was 1.6 inches (4 cm) longer, 0.8 inches (2 cm) narrower, and 1.6 inches (4 cm) lower. For the first two years, it had a 479 cc, 15 HP engine. In 1959, the engine power was increased to 17 HP without increasing the displacement. Beginning in 1960, the 449.5 cc engine of the D was used in the Bianchina, and the Special, a two-toned version with an 18 HP engine, was produced.

86-87 THIS REAR VIEW OF A BASIC THIRD SERIES TRASFORMABILE MADE, FOR EXPORTATION HIGHLIGHTS, THE FABRIC TOP BETWEEN METAL SIDE PANELS, LIKE THE 500, AND THE DESIGN OF THE ROSTRUMS THAT SERVED AS BUMPER ENDS.

87 TOP THE LONGER, SQUARER ROOF THAT CHARACTERIZED THE 1962 BERLINA SEDAN MADE IT POSSIBLE FOR FOUR PASSENGERS TO RIDE IN COMFORT. THE FRONT HOOD AND THE TRUNK WERE BOXIER THAN THOSE OF THE TRASFORMABILE.

87 BOTTOM THIS CABRIOLET WAS CREATED IN 1960 AS THE EVOLUTION OF A ONE-OFF UNIT MANUFACTURED IN 1959. THE BUMPERS WRAPPED SLIGHTLY AROUND THE SIDES. ITS DOOR WINDOWS HAD NEITHER PILLARS NOR FRAMES.

In 1960, the Cabriolet was born, with restyled front and back ends, sleeker lines, and no fixed B-pillars. The only thing that jutted from the beltline was the windshield, and the passenger compartment was covered by a classic convertible top in fabric over a ribbed structure. The new lines of the front end and hood would be used in the subsequent four-seater sedan. An original hard top was available to protect the passenger compartment during wet and cold seasons. It was built using the mechanics of both the 500 D and the 500 F, with the passage from one to the other occurring in 1965, obviously. The Trasformabile went out of production in 1962, when it was replaced by the four-seater sedan with a 499 cc, 17 HP engine in the regular version and a 21 HP engine in the Special version, which was characterized by its two-toned exterior and better-finished interior. The sedan was based on the Cabriolet and had its same beltline and front and rear hoods. Its interior comfort was noticeably better than that of the Trasformabile, but its sleeker lines made it less appealing: tastes had changed a lot from the end of the '50s to the beginning of the '60s, and many thought it looked pretentious. The final blow to its image began in 1975 (the Bianchina was already out of production) when the actor Paolo Villaggio chose the Bianchina as the car for his meek, tragicomic character, Ugo Fantozzi. When the 500 F arrived in 1965, the Bianchina underwent its mechanical retrofitting. The sedan and Cabriolet got an 18 HP engine, while the Special stayed at 21 HP. Production was halted in 1969.

A parallel production of the Bianchina took place in Germany, at the Karosseriewerke Weinsberg, where semi-complete 500s began to arrive in 1959. The two models produced reflected German tastes at the time, meaning they had lines inspired by great cars, even though the country was still weak from the war and its resources did not match the desires of its population. The NSU-Fiat Weinsberg 500 Coupé was a two-seater with rather pronounced fins that were reminiscent of the 1500L-1800-2100, a wrap-around back window, and a triangular rear pillar. The Limousette, on the other hand, was a berlinetta or little 2 + 2 sedan that combined the original top of the 500 with tailfins. Both models were two-toned, one color for the roof and one for the beltline and the hoods. A second series of the Limousette was produced on the base of the 500 D in 1960, with the same two-toned finish and a band on the beltline that matched the roof. The second series had a new brand name: it was no longer NSU-Fiat but Neckar, the name of the new company born after legal disputes arose between Fiat and NSU, where production had begun again with the Prinz in 1958. From 1959 to 1963, approximately 6,200 Weinsbergs were manufactured.

88   THE FRONT END OF THE LIMOUSETTE IS REMINISCENT OF THE BIGGER SEDANS, THE 1500L, 1800, AND 2100, ALL OF WHICH WERE ALSO PRODUCED IN 1959. THE BIG GRILLE AND MOUSTACHE WINGS SIMULATE THE PRESENCE OF A RADIATOR.

88-89 AS SMALL AS IT WAS, THE LIMOUSETTE WAS A TRUE THREE-BOXES SEDAN, WITH THE ENGINE IN THE BACK. ITS TAIL FINS WERE REMINISCENT OF THE 1957 GRANLUCE 1200.

A LONG DRESS FOR BUSINESS: 500 GIARDINIERA AND FURGONCINO (1960–1977)

Fiat's engineering department began designing a work version of the 500 sedan, with its 68.5-inch (1,740 mm) wheelbase, almost immediately. The 600 Multipla that replaced the 500 C Belvedere was not as successful as its designers had expected it to be, despite its courageous esthetics—which, thirty years after it went out of production, would make the car a design icon and the first mass-produced van in the world—and despite the fact that the market was in need of a small station wagon that could also be a small van. The first design attempts were made using the frame of an elongated 500 sedan and produced at least one four-seater prototype and one van, with the brand name Autobianchi. Both had a large side door; but with the vertically mounted engine, there was no access to the rear of the vehicle. This prompted Giacosa's team to design a flat engine, a solution that had recently been adopted by Fiat for its coaches. The transmission and radiator stayed in their original positions; but the crankcase, lubrication system, clutch, and housing for the starter motor were redesigned. It had a 499.5 cc engine, the same displacement as the Sport, which would soon be used for the 500 D and subsequent models. It was the most powerful engine ever mounted on a 500 (21.5 HP) and, in fact, it was used for the single-seater in the Formula 875 Monza race. The horizontal engine in the 120, as the new project was called internally, made it possible to mount a hinged rear door for access to the cargo area. The brakes and suspension were sized for heavier loads, but they followed the sedan layout. It had a 72.4-inch (1,840 mm) wheelbase, 3.9 inches (10 cm) more than the sedan. In May 1960, sales of the 120 began. It was named the 500 Giardiniera and sold for 565,000 ITL.

90-91 THE FIRST VERSION OF THE GIARDINIERA CAME OUT IN 1960. ITS MOLDINGS AND WHITEWALL TIRES GAVE IT LESS OF AN INEVITABLE WORK-VEHICLE LOOK.

A commercial version was added alongside the Giardiniera: the Furgoncino (van), which was manufactured using the same body but without the two back seats and back windows. The Giardiniera and Furgoncino incorporated bodywork changes that would be introduced a few months later in the 500 D and that maintained the characteristics of the D, particularly its suicide doors, which were not yet banned in vans. In March 1965, production was transferred from Mirafiori to Desio. The moldings halfway up the sides were eliminated, the hubcaps of the 850 replaced those of the 500 D, and the interior was updated to that of the 500 F.

In 1969, with the same body, the car received the Autobianchi trademark, which was initially a small grille like the one on the Bianchina sedan, and later, the Autobianchi badge in the holder used for the Fiat emblem for the 500 F second series and the L. Ultimately, an elongated version was created to fit in the diamond-shaped holder of the 500 R. The Giardiniera outlasted the 500 R by a year and a half. When it went out of production in 1977, after a total of 327,000 units produced—140,000 first series, 75,000 Fiat second series in Desio, and 112,000 with the Autobianchi trademark—it still had its 499.5 cc engine and its suicide doors.

92 CUTAWAY DRAWING OF THE 500 GIARDINIERA. ITS HORIZONTAL MOTOR WAS UNDER THE FLOOR, WHICH WAS PARTICULARLY CLOSE TO THE GROUND IN THE CARGO COMPARTMENT.

93 THE SUNROOF OF THE 500 GIARDINIERA WAS IN FABRIC LIKE THAT OF THE SEDAN. IT OPENED THE PART OF THE ROOF ABOVE THE FRONT AND BACK SEATS.

AN ELEGANT WORKER: THE BIANCHINA PANORAMICA AND FURGONCINO (1960-1969)

94-95 THE BIANCHINA PANORAMICA WAS AVAILABLE WITH THE SAME SUNROOF AS THE 500 GIARDINIERA OR WITH A COMPLETELY METAL ROOF, LIKE THE ONE IN THE PHOTO.

95 THE VAN VERSION WAS AVAILABLE WITH A LOW ROOF (A PANORAMICA WITH THE SIDE WINDOWS BLACKED OUT) OR WITH A HIGH ROOF AND A CUBE-SHAPED CARGO COMPARTMENT, WHICH BECAME VERY COMMON IN THE 1970S.

Autobianchi used a 1940 wheelbase and a 110 flat engine to make the Bianchina Panoramica, the station-wagon version, available with a hardtop or sunroof and a rear, top-hinged door, not right-hinged like that of the 500 Giardiniera. It had the same front body as that of the Cabriolet and, like the sedan, was available with a regular solid-color finish or in the Special version that was two-toned with a contrasting colored roof. The engine in all versions was a 499.5 cc, 21 HP flat engine. Its refined finishes took the Panoramica's image beyond that of a work vehicle, an image that even the most prestigious station wagons were having trouble shaking off at the time. It became a valid alternative for those who were looking for a fuel-efficient four-seater.

In addition to the Panoramica, Autobianchi produced a high-roof and low-roof van, two very different versions. The low-roof version was based on the Panoramica but had no side windows in the back, while the high-roof version introduced Italy to a previously unseen type of cargo vehicle: a small van with a back "cube," the same that would become famous on the Fiat Fiorino. Diffusion of both versions was limited, despite the important commissions that Autobianchi received from public institutions, such as the postal service. The Panoramica went out of production in 1969 and was replaced by the already-mentioned Autobianchi Giardiniera, derived from the body of the 500 Giardiniera, which was already being produced in Desio.

TOPLESS ON THE BEACH: GHIA JOLLY (1957–1962)

In 1955, Ghia used the chassis of a Fiat 600 to create the Jolly, a completely open to-be-used-on-the-seaside vehicle with no doors that, at the most, had a surrey top to protect its passengers from the sun. A more successful model using a 500 chassis was proposed in 1957. Jollys had tubular front bumpers and many of the features of the mass-produced vehicles, but their passenger compartments were cut and had no doors, their doorsills were reinforced and approximately 8 inches (20 cm) higher than usual, and their seats were made of rattan.

The front end of the very first Jolly was a bit different; but the subsequent mass-produced series used the original.

Jollys based on the 500, 500 D, and 500 F were the most common, but similar transformations were made to the 500 Giardiniera, the Bianchina, and the 600 Berlina and Multipla. A version with protruding headlights was made for the North American market. The Jolly was an international success, a social phenomenon, indispensable in luxury hotels. It was this success that led to the creation of a simpler version of the Jolly, the Thailandia, made by cutting complete vehicles down, rather than fitting out bare frames. The French Tplv produced a similar but less esthetically pleasing vehicle.

96 AND 97 THIS JOLLY WITH A NUOVA 500 BASE HAD NON-STANDARD FEATURES THAT INCLUDED PADDED RATHER THAN RATTAN SEATS AND A GRILLE THAT COVERED THE AIR INTAKE VENTS. THE LICENSE PLATE IN THE PHOTO IS AMERICAN, BUT THE MODEL IS EUROPEAN.

Z, AS IN . . . ZAGATO ZANZARA (1969)

The Zanzara was created in 1969, a difficult period for sports cars. Its body was a nod to the dune buggy that was particularly popular at the time. It had the low, sleek front end of a sports car, curved with no bumpers, but the rest of the body resembled that of an off-road beach car: its rear engine hood was the same height as the top of the windshield.

It had no doors, and the seats were lower than the very low-slung sides, allowing passengers to climb into the car. The protruding fenders were joined in the back by a kind of shelf that jutted out of the hood. The Hondina Youngstar, created on a Honda N360 frame, was based on Ercole Spada's design; it was very similar to the Zanzara, but its headlights were rectangular rather than round. Both of the two Zanzaras produced were built on a 500 F frame; one was red, and the other was green.

98-99 ONLY ITS WHEEL SIZE AND WHEELBASE REVEALED THAT THIS ZANZARA WAS A DERIVATION OF THE 500. THE HEIGHT OF THE TRUNK IN THE BACK WAS ONLY A MATTER OF ESTHETICS.

99 A ZANZARA, PROBABLY THE GREEN ONE, WITH A FEW SMALL DETAILS THAT DISTINGUISH IT FROM THE ONE ON THE BOTTOM. THE GAS TANK AND SPARE TIRE WERE UNDER THE HOOD.

Success without fame:
126, Cinquecento and Seicento

126: la più _giovane_ delle piccole Fia

100-101 THIS ILLUSTRATION FOR THE FIRST VERSION OF THE
126, WITH CHROME BUMPERS AND THE SAME WHEELS AS THE
500 R, AS IT EMERGES FROM A DREAMLIKE SETTING, IS VERY
EARLY '70S. THE YELLOW IS REMINISCENT OF THE POSITANO
YELLOW OF THE 500, FIRST USED IN 1968.

In 1968, with the F in production and the L newly launched on the market, Fiat began thinking about a substitute for the 500. Inspiration arrived from the studio of Pio Manzù, the son of the sculptor Giacomo Manzù, and the designer who had worked with Alessi, Flos, and Kartell. He was called as a consultant to Dante Giacosa's Centro Stile Fiat to direct the development of the 127, which he never lived to see; he lost his life in an auto accident on the Turin-Milan tollway the night before the mockup was to be presented. Manzù's showcar was based on an

850 Idroconvert platform; with lines so taut that they were shaped with a putty knife in the plaster models. Dante Giacosa followed the first two years of development full-time before he reached retirement age in 1970, so the 126, born in 1972 with the difficult task of replacing the already iconic 500, would not have a famous name to bolster its image. A rumor circulated maintaining that the 126 had actually been conceived by the new generation: its intent was to underline the end of the era of Giacosa; but the rumors were proved untrue, on one hand by the dates and on the other by two precise and plausible reasons to replace the 500. The first was the need to introduce a structure with varying energy absorption, with crumple zones and a safety cell (features that would soon be imposed by new safety standards), something that would not be possible with the 1957 structure. Secondly, Fiat needed a model in step with the times, not one that was fifteen years old, to expand into socialist countries, together with the Zastava, which had been in production in Yugoslavia since 1953; the Lada/Shigulì made in Togliatti's Russian factory since 1975; and the Polski Fiat 125p, manufactured by the Polish FSO since 1967. The agreement for the new vehicle was signed with the government-owned Polish company, Pol-Mot, on October 29, 1971. The new

101 PRODUCTION OF THE 126 IN CASSINO. A PARALLEL PRODUCTION BEGAN AT APPROXIMATELY THE SAME TIME IN THE BIELSKO-BIALA FACTORY IN POLAND, JUST AS THE SIMCA CINQ AND THEN THE 500 STEYR-PUCH HAD BEEN MANUFACTURED IN A CONCURRENT PRODUCTION IN A FOREIGN COUNTRY.

company created to build the 126 in Poland was the FSM (Fabryka Samochodów Małolitrażowych, meaning "small-engine car factory"). The Polski Fiat brand continued to be used for the 125p and the short-lived 127p. On November 9, 1972, the 126 was presented simultaneously in Via Roma in Turin and in Defilad Square in Warsaw. Polish production began on June 6, 1973, with CKD (completely knocked-down, or disassembled) vehicles sent from Cassino. Later, production became completely local.

SQUARE-SHAPED SIMPLICITY: THE 126 I SERIES (1972–1977)

The mechanics of the Italian and Polish versions were identical, based on the evolution of the 500 engine that reached 594 cc and delivered 16kW/23 HP; its gearbox remained a 4-speed, but it was synchronized. The gas tank was moved from the trunk in the front to the back, for safety reasons, and although the wheelbase remained the same as its precursor, the body was bigger. Only one trim package and one engine were available but there were two options for the roof, which could be completely closed or with a sunroof that opened above the front seat, like the roof of the 1959 500. In September 1975, the Tychy factory joined the Bielsko-Biała factory, both of which were located in the Silesia region, in Polish production. Four FSM versions were made in that period: the 126p 600 (standard model), the 600S (special version), the 600K (Comfort), and the 600I (outfitted for disabled drivers). In Austria, the heir to the 500 Steyr-Puch was a 126 made with bodies sent

from Cassino, which were completed with Steyr axles and a 25 HP 643 cc two-cylinder boxer. Production lasted for two years.

The 126 got its first restyling in November 1976, which meant three versions for Western Europe. The Base kept the chrome bumpers from the first series; the Personal had an upgraded interior that included a dashboard covered in carpet that would later be replaced with imitation leather, but a rather austere back bench; and the Personal 4 was identical to the Personal, but with a padded back seat. The Personal was called the De Ville in Great Britain and the Bambino in Germany. All of the versions had an alternator instead of a dynamo, new wheels with black plastic hubcaps, and 40 rather than 48 air vents in the hood. The space for the license plate was changed from vertical to horizontal to accommodate the new shapes of the plates that were being issued in the European Economic Community at the time.

102 THE CASSINO FIRST SERIES HAD ORANGE INDICATOR LIGHTS AND STILL HAD THE CHROME BUMPERS THAT WERE USED IN POLAND ON SOME VERSIONS UNTIL THE LATE 1980S.

103 THE RANGE OF COLORS OF THE 126 FIRST SERIES HAD SOME COLORS IN COMMON WITH THE 500 R. THE CLOSED-ROOF VERSION WAS THE MOST WIDELY REQUESTED IN ITALY.

UP TO DATE DETAILS: 126 II SERIES (1977–1987)

104-105 THE BLACK WAS ONE OF THE FIRST TWO SPECIALS BASED ON THE 126 PERSONAL 4. THE TAILLIGHT GROUP WITH A BACKUP LIGHT WAS AN EXCLUSIVE FEATURE IN THE FOUR VERSIONS NAMED FOR COLORS.

105 THE RED (WHICH WAS AN AMARANTH RED) AND THE BROWN (WHICH WAS A VERY DARK BROWN), BASED ON THE SECOND SERIES PRODUCED IN POLAND, REPLICATED THE SUCCESS OF THE BLACK AND THE SILVER.

In the second series, a 652 cc engine replaced the 594 in Western Europe in July 1977, but the trim packages remained the same. The 594 cc engine remained on the market in Poland for another year, alongside the new one in all four versions (650, 650S, 650K, 650I). Its headlights were updated to those of the 127 Second Series, with incorporated parking lights and without the double-filament bulb, which had been used for both parking lights and front turn signals.

The following year, the first two special (but not limited) versions of the Personal 4 appeared, with the trim packages of the Personal 4 of the first series. With newly added elegance and refinement, it aimed to court the female audience and assume the role of second family car. The two versions were the Black and the Silver, with pastel paint colors to match their names, and both had logos and contrasting side stripes. Interior upholstery was more refined and was color-coordinated with the body. The taillight unit included a backup light.

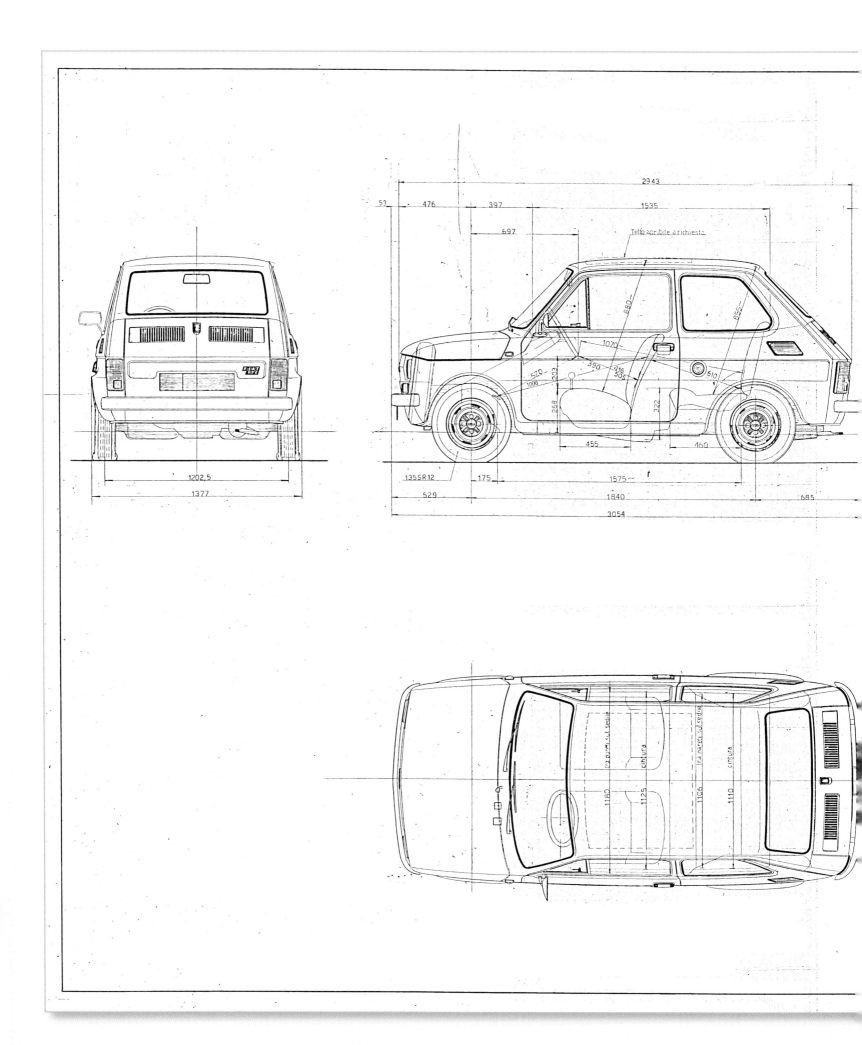

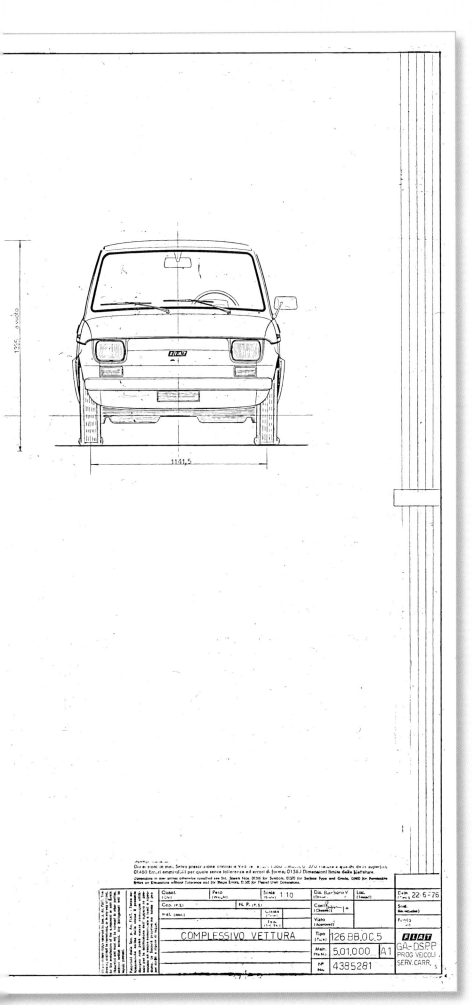

After 1979, the left-hand-drive 126s would no longer be produced in Bielsko-Biała or in Italy, where they had been manufactured in Cassino (FR), Desio (MB), and Termini Imerese (PA). They would all be produced in Tychy, including the new 1980 special series Red (which was a dark liver red) and Brown (which was dark brown) that replaced the Silver and Black with new chrome details and coordinated fabric and imitation leather upholstery. The right-hand-drive versions, very much in demand in the U.K., were only available with a sunroof. They were produced until 1983 at the Sicilfiat plant. CKD kits from Silesia also arrived in Kragujevac (at the time Yugoslavia, now Serbia) that were assembled and sold with the Zastava brand. The car was nicknamed "Peglica," meaning "little iron." Sale of the 126 began again in Europe in 1983. Only one version was available, the 126 Unificata, which would remain in production until 1985. Its trim package was equivalent to that of the Personal 4 with restyled, more form-fitting bumpers. In 1984, the 126p also upgraded to the new esthetics. In 1983, the 126.A1.076 engine was created, solely for Eastern European markets, with redesigned heads that were adapted for 87-octane gasoline. The models it was used in were called the 650E, ES, EK, or EI, depending on the trim package. Between the end of 1984 and the beginning of 1985, the 126 Unificata and the 126p got a new dashboard, rearview mirror, and backup lights, in addition to rear fog lights suspended under the back bumper. In observance of a European law that required informing the customer of a product's origin, the back shield read "Made by FSM." It came to be known as the "126 FSM" among specialists, even though it was not the first to be produced by the Polish factory. The 126 was exported to all of Western Europe (sold by the network of Fiat dealerships) and to Eastern Europe, as well as to Australia (where it was called the FSM Niki), Cuba, Cyprus, and Egypt. When, in an experimental move, 23,000 126s were sent to China (to the Wenzhou region) for the first time in 1980, they gave many private citizens the opportunity to own a car, and to some even to start their own taxi business. In fact, 5,000 of the 126s became taxis in the capital city.

106–107 THE SECOND SERIES HAD THE SAME WHEELS AS THE LAST UNITS OF THE FIRST SERIES, A LONG LICENSE-PLATE FRAME, AND BLACK PLASTIC BUMPERS.

EVOLVED GENERATIONS: THE 126 BIS, MALUCH, AND GIANNINI RACERS (1987-2000)

An important but nearly invisible revolution in 1987 led to the creation of the 126 Bis. The car was developed over a two-year period by Polish designers, who were supervised by the engineers in Turin. Its engine was rotated horizontally, like that of the Giardiniera, but it was water-cooled. The engine was increased to 703 cc and delivered 18 kW/25 HP. There were no fewer than 800 differences between the Bis and its predecessor, but almost all of them were only slightly visible. Only one stood out: thanks to its flat engine, the Bis had a rear hatchback and a 29-gallon (110-liter) trunk. For the first time since the days of the 500, the size of the wheels changed, to 12" instead of 13". In order to stay on the market for a few more years, this was a necessary update, but it got a lukewarm reception in Western Europe as well as in Poland, where it was uncommon. The Bis was in production until 1989, but slightly fewer than 191,000 were manufactured. In the last two years of production, it became the Bis Up; the only difference between the two versions was the side decals.

The 126p vertical engine continued to be the best seller in Western Europe. To simplify production, the 126p was manufactured in only one version (the Standard, which still had steel bumpers, went out of production), which was updated with the same back fenders as the Bis. Modifications made in 1990 included a new carburetor, an inertia switch that shut off the fuel pump in an accident, and a new but still electromechanical ignition. In 1993, when the FSM became Fiat Auto Poland, it was 90% controlled by the Fiat parent company in Italy. In 1994, body molds were redesigned and the electronic ignition was introduced, giving birth to a version that had a completely smooth beltline, something Western Europe was not familiar with. It was called the 126 EL or EL SX, depending on the trim package. It had the Cinquecento's rearview mirror, steering wheel, and gearshift and no door guards. Bosmal, a public company that was born as a spinoff of FSM's research and development department, developed prototypes and produced autos on a small scale. Using the EL, Bosmal built 507 units of a 126 Cabriolet, a convertible with a roll bar, a few of which made it to Italy through an independent importer. In December 1996, the EL and the EL SX were replaced by the 126 ELX, which was homologated as a Euro 1, thanks to its electronic fuel injection system and its catalytic muffler.

In 1998, Poland's nickname for the 126, "Maluch," meaning baby, was officially added to the name, written in playful colored letters on the side, the same used by Valentino Rossi to write "The Doctor" on the side of his number 46.

108-109 WHILE OTHER EUROPEAN MARKETS WERE SELLING THE 126 BIS WITH A FLAT ENGINE AND HATCHBACK, POLAND WAS SELLING THIS VERSION WITH A VERTICAL MOTOR. THE BUMPERS WITH A WIDE LICENSE PLATE FRAME, THE SIDE STRIPS, AND THE HUBCAPS WERE THE SAME AS THOSE ON THE BIS. IT WAS THE LAST MODEL PRODUCED WITH THE POLSKI FIAT NAME.

110-111 THANKS TO ITS HORIZONTAL ENGINE, THE 126 BIS HAD A HATCHBACK AND BACK TRUNK. THE SIDE STRIPS WERE THE SAME AS THOSE ON THE EARLIER MODEL, THE 126 UNIFICATA.

111 THE 126 BIS UP WAS THE LAST MODEL SOLD IN ITALY. THE ONLY FEATURE THAT DISTINGUISHED IT FROM THE FIRST BIS WERE THE BLACK AND BLUE STICKERS (THE SAME FOR EVERY COLOR CAR) ON THE FRONT AND SIDES.

The Maluch no longer had the Polski Fiat brand: it had a five-bar Fiat logo. The Town, a more accessorized version that could be identified by its back headrests, became available in addition to the basic version. There was still a demand for the new Maluch in 2000, but the run-down conditions of the production lines and the high cost of producing new body molds led Fiat to halt production. In September 2000, two numbered limited editions of 500 units each, the Maluch Happy End in yellow and red, celebrated the end of a career that had lasted 17 years and had produced 4,680,155 units, 1,359,912 built in Italy, 3,318,674 in Poland, and 2,069 in Austria.

No racing 126s were made in Italy. When the 126 was born, Abarth was too busy with racecars, rallies and records to take notice; and in the following decade, the appeal of the compact car had already worn off. The only tuning company to produce a series of the sporting version of the 126 was Giannini Automobili,

a company that was transformed when the lawyer Volfango Polverelli arrived in the early '70s. He was initially called upon to reorganize the company, later becoming a partner and then the new owner. He replaced the carburetor and the spark plugs and revised every element that could increase performance. His many improvements included the head, high-compression pistons, polished and swaged ducts, increased cylinder capacity, larger cylinder beds, balanced counterweighted crankshaft, fixed camshaft, balanced connecting rods, and a bigger, lighter oil pan. The first version maintained the original engine size (594 cc); the 650, 700, and 800 cc engines followed. Few modifications were made to the bodies of the Gianninis; at most, a decoration or decal on the front or side identified the version as one made by the Roman tuning company. The models were called GP, GPA, GPS, NP, or NPA, depending on the level of tuning. The GP and GPS could be built on both the 126 and the Personal.

112 AND 113 IN 1995, THE YOUNG BECAME THE BASIC VERSION OF THE 500 II SERIES, REPLACING THE S. THE CHEERFUL COLORS OF THE UPHOLSTERY BRIGHTENED THE BASIC TRIM PACKAGE. AIRBAGS WERE AN OPTIONAL FEATURE.

In 1991, when Jaruzelski resigned his post as president of the new republic and Poland became a democracy with a liberal economy once again, production of the replacement for the 126 finally began. Its name, Cinquecento (meaning five hundred) written in letters, alluded to its iconic ancestor. It was a simple, not-very-modern hatchback designed by Ermanno Cressoni and Antonio Piovano, with an interior by Claudio Mottino and Giuseppe Bortolusso. Engine choices were the 704 cc horizontal water-cooled twin-cylinder of the 126 bis, or the 903 cc four-cylinder 100 series, used for the first time on the 1965 850 Coupé but derived from that of the 600 ten years earlier. The Cinquecento had a front-wheel-drive front engine or a "tutto avanti," and it was the first Fiat produced exclusively in Poland. For the first two years, it was sold with the Fiat brand for exportation and with the FSM brand on the Polish market, where it never achieved great success because of its high price. The 704 that powered the Cinquecento ED (Economy Drive) delivered 31 HP at 5,000 rpm and took it to a maximum speed of 80 miles per hour (128 kph), while the 41 HP 903 cc that went on the market at the beginning of 1992 reached a maximum speed of 87 miles per hour (140 kph). The ED reintroduced the dashboard of the 126 bis. It had no headrests (except in Poland). Its black (rather than matching) bumpers, its hubcaps that covered only the center of the wheel, and its visible gas cap made it recognizable from the outside. The first series went out of production in 1993, making the 903 the rarest Cinquecento of all. The mild restyling that took place in 1993 brought a smaller Fiat logo and catalytic converters in compliance with Euro 1 regulations, and a Japanese Aisan carburetor for the twin cylinder. The four-cylinder adopted single-

FAST FORWARD: CINQUECENTO I AND II SERIES (1991–1998)

point electronic injection and reduced the size of the engine to 899 cc for tax and insurance issues. There was still only one trim package available per model; the two cylinder was updated with a new selection of colors for upholstery and plastic details and a fuel door for the gas cap. In 1994, the range was extended, with three versions for the 899 with a synchronized 5-gear transmission and 155/65 R13 tires. The bumpers, mirrors, and door handles were in black plastic on the S and matched the body color on the SX. The headlights and taillights on the SX were monochrome, white in the front and red in the back, without the orange of the turn signals. The Suite was an SX with air conditioning, a rare element in a car of its size at the time. The SX and the Suite offered a range of options that included power windows, double

rearview mirror, a central locking system, and an automatic trunk opener. The Young, which was introduced in 1995 to replace the S, offered an optional airbag for the driver. The year's entire range was proposed with new upholstery and wider rims. The 1996 Soleil (called Sole on some foreign markets) had a power sunroof. The Van was introduced exclusively on the Polish and Spanish markets in 1998. It was a tiny van with a 259-gallon (980-liter) trunk and a 771-pound (350-kg) load capacity powered by an 899 cc fuel-injected engine. It was also in 1998 that the Cinquecento's career ended, after 1,102,684 units had been produced. At that point, the passion for mechanical tuning had waned, and anyone who wanted a racy Cinquecento would have to settle for the excellent performance of the Sporting.

ENVIRONMENT, RACES, AND CREATIVITY: THE CINQUECENTO SPORTING, ELETTRA, AND THE SPECIAL BODIES (1994–1997)

In 1994, on the base of the first series, the racer Sporting came out. It had an 1108 cc Fire series engine that delivered 54 HP at 5,500 rpm and a speed of 98 miles per hour (158 kph); it was the engine of the Punto 55, combined with the transmission of the Uno 1000. A new front anti-roll bar adapted the car's handling to its speed. The Sporting could be identified by a number of elements: its special colors, including the iconic Giallo Ginestra, a kind of canary yellow, commonly seen in the Coupé and Barchetta; black; Sporting red; and metallic gray; mirrors, door handles, and bumpers that matched the body color; bumper moldings in a contrasting color; and dark taillights. The interior had comfortable, form-fitting seats, a leather-covered steering wheel and gearshift, red seatbelts, and special instruments. Options available included air-conditioning, split back seats, a spoiler on the hatchback, a radio with removable front panel, and door guards. Production of the Sporting continued with a second series. In 1997, the spoiler on the Sporting was fitted with a third brake light, and an Abarth esthetic tuning kit became available for the British market. New colors added were Starter red, Trend gray, and Imola blue. The Elettra, an electric version with lead-gel or nickel-cadmium batteries, was available throughout the Cinque-cento's career. The Cinquecento with a lead-gel battery weighed 500 pounds (1,100 kg); it had a range of 45 miles (70 km) in the city and 62 miles (100 km) on the highway; its battery lasted for 600 charge cycles. With nickel-cadmium batteries, it weighed 462 pounds (1,020 kg) and had a range of 62 miles (100 km) in the city and 93 miles (150 km) on the highway; the battery lifespan was 1,800 charge cycles. It had front-wheel drive and the same trim package as the S.

Only three modifications worth mentioning were made to the body. Coriasco included the details of the Style series of the Tempra, the Tipo, and the Uno on its version of the Sporting. Giannini, who for once did not modify the kinematic chain, limited its changes to a personalization of the interior (very few were produced, all in 1993 with a 903 engine). Terberg, a specialized truck builder in the Netherlands, created a small Cinquecento cabriolet that maintained its classically shaped front doors, making the vehicle look like a pickup from the side. The lines the body was cut along were capped with black plastic. The open portion could be closed with a normal convertible top with side windows, or with a sort of tonneau that covered the back seats.

114-115 THE LOOK OF THE SPORTING DEPENDED ON ITS VIVACIOUS COLORS, LIKE SPORTING RED AND SCOTCH BROOM YELLOW, AND VERY SIMPLE CUSTOMIZATION. IT HAD A 1,108 CC FIRE ENGINE.

115 DUE TO THE SIZE OF ITS BATTERY, THE 500 ELETTRA HAD ONLY TWO FRONT SEATS. IT HAD A FIVE-SPEED TRANSMISSION, AND THE MOTOR WAS IN THE FRONT.

The Seicento replaced the Cinquecento; it was presented in September 1997 and went on the market at the time of the 1998 Geneva Auto Show. Fundamentally, it was the same as the Cinquecento with a stiffer structure, especially in the uprights and front wheel arches, for better shock resistance. Its rounder design was in step with the times, and its sloping front end made it a little longer at 10.9 feet (3.34 m). Esthetic updates, which regarded primarily the shape of the headlights, the back side windows, and the rear window, were the work of Luciano Bove and Luciano Speranza from the Centro Stile Fiat. The interior was restyled by Giuseppe Bortolusso, the designer of the interior of the Cinquecento. The Seicento was also powered by a choice of the 899 cc "100 series," used in the S and SX versions as well as in the Citymatic that had an automatic clutch, or the Fire 1108, the engine of the Suite and the Sporting. All versions had an electronic fuel-injection system and catalytic converter, and Euro 2 homologation, as well as an immobilizer and seatbelts with pretensioners. The SX also had the usual wheels, mirrors, and bumpers that matched the body, doors that were completely lined internally, a special instrument panel and gearshift, and an anti-roll bar. Like the previous version, the Suite had air-conditioning, but it also featured electric power steering, black pillars, and a gearshift that was different from the SX's. The Van version, built on the S, came out immediately. It was powered by an 899 or 1108 cc engine, and its back side windows and rear window were covered with blackout film. It had the same size cargo area as the Cinquecento (259 gallons), but its load capacity was 230 pounds (505 kg). The S went out of production in January 1999, replaced by the Young, which was slightly better equipped, with an 899 or 1108 cc

engine, and was less expensive. It was called Mia in the U.K. and was offered with only the 899 cc engine. In the same period, the Hobby was offered with the same equipment as the SX and a central locking system. The Olimpia was a similar model with a standard equipment radio/CD player that came out in Poland in 2000. In November, the Fun went on the market. It was a pastel yellow or metallic blue Young with matching bumpers. Abarth made a non-homologated version that was destined only for the racetrack. It was a 6-speed with a Viscodrive differential, a reinforced frame, four disc brakes, and a 115 HP 1143 cc Fire engine.

116 AND 117 THE BASIC SEICENTO HAD BLACK BUMPERS, ITS LUGNUTS WERE ON THE CENTER OF THE WHEELS, AND ITS UPHOLSTERY COLORS WERE SIMILAR TO THOSE OF THE CINQUECENTO YOUNG.

SPORT, STYLE, AND ENVIRONMENT: THE SEICENTO II SERIES, SPORTING, SPORTING MICHAEL SCHUMACHER, BRUSH, ELETTRA (2000–2005)

An electric version was immediately in the works with the same name as the electric Cinquecento, Elettra. It was a rear-wheel drive with a 30 kW motor and four seats, thanks to the fact that its eighteen 60 Ah batteries were less bulky than those of its precursor (the batteries were lead-acid again). The Elettra was manufactured by the ex-Alfa Romeo plant in Arese with semi-complete cars that arrived from Tychy.

In 2000, the second series, homologated Euro 3, was the first to offer only one engine choice, the Fire, which for the occasion adopted multipoint injection. New elements included the instrument panel, the upholstery, the gearshift (the same as that of the Suite), and the white plastic on the turn signals. The Fiat logo was the 100th anniversary logo introduced the previous year, with a laurel wreath around a circle with a blue background. The Citymatic transmission was eliminated, and the trim packages were S, SX, and Sporting, all with the same equipment

as that of the first series. An S with slightly updated equipment was sold as the EL (marketed with the name Team in Germany). Completely new names arrived with the 2002 range. The Base became the old S, the Comfort became the SX (but with standard equipment electric power steering), and the Suite became the Clima. The name changes were an indication of the change in the Seicento's image, no longer trendy and fun but serious and substantial. For the Polish market, there were the Go!, an SX with the side moldings of the latest Sporting and a standard equipment radio; the Dynamic (2003), with power windows and a driver's seat airbag; and the Look, with a driver's-seat airbag and electric power steering. In 2004, the Base became the Actual, the Comfort became the Active, and the production of Seicentos with right-hand drive was halted.

118 THE SPECIAL COLORS OF THE SEICENTO SPORTING'S UPHOLSTERY ACCENTUATED ITS SPORTY LOOK. AIR-CONDITIONING WAS AN OPTIONAL FEATURE.

118-119 THE SEICENTO SPORTING'S DISTINGUISHING FEATURES WERE THE SHIELD ON THE FRONT BUMPER, ALLOY WHEELS, AND SIDE SKIRTS, AS WELL AS ITS SPECIAL COLOR RANGE THAT INCLUDED THE ICONIC SCOTCH BROOM YELLOW.

Produced in 2001 on the base of the second series, the special two-toned version, Brush (called 2Tone in the U.K.) introduced contrasting colored hatchback, bumpers, and side guards in orange, green, and blue color combinations. The Brush Plus trim package included electric power steering, a central locking system, and a convertible top.

The souped-up version of the Seicento was created with the first series. It was called Sporting, like previous versions, and had light-alloy wheels, a speedometer,

and a special gear ratio. ABS, air-conditioning, and electric power steering were optional. An Abarth kit was available that shortened the third, fourth, and fifth gears and added bigger wheels. In addition to the Sporting, there was special numbered Michael Schumacher version. Originally, the edition was supposed to be limited to 1,000 units, but at least 2,500 units were actually produced. Added equipment included power steering, an anti-roll bar, a central locking system, a driver's-seat airbag, ABS, two-toned seats, aluminum pedals, and, obviously, a numbered plaque and the Michael Schumacher logo. Air-conditioning was optional. In 2004, the Sporting followed the declining trend of the model and went out of production.

120-121 THE MICHAEL SCHUMACHER EDITION OF THE SEICENTO SPORTING HAD HIS LOGO ON THE HATCHBACK AND A NUMBERED PLAQUE ON THE SIDE SKIRTS.

121 THE BATTERY PACK OF THE SEICENTO ELETTRA WAS MORE COMPACT THAN THAT OF THE CINQUECENTO.

The third series, which included the versions Actual and Active, was presented in 2005. Its name, 600 written in numbers rather than letters, was reminiscent of the 1995 model, as was its front badge holder. The special 50th Anniversary version was added to the range with the third series. Its colors were reminiscent of the first 600: light blue, cream, sage green, and gray-blue. The seats bore the Fiat logo in elongated capital letters, the same logo that was used for a very fashionable clothing line, thanks to a brilliant idea of Lapo Elkann. But not even standard equipment that included ABS and EBD on the entire range was enough to change the 600's deplorable results in the Euro NCAP tests. After all, the structure was a project from 1991; in 2008 the model disappeared from all European markets except Italy and Poland. The last model year, 2009, included the Actual and Active with electric power steering, a central locking system, power windows, and the seats from the 50th Anniversary edition. In 2010, the 600 was taken off the market to make room on the production lines for the higher-than-estimated demand for the 500, launched in 2017, and for the second series of Ka that Fiat was producing for Ford on the 500 base. A total of 1,281,087 units were produced, of which 724,000 were destined to Italy, almost 290,000 to Poland, 82,000 to Germany, 46,000 to the U.K., and 33,000 each for Spain, Greece, and the Netherlands. There was also a small series of electric models with fuel cells, a type of clean energy derived from aerospace technology that combines oxygen and hydrogen molecules to produce the electricity that powers the motor. Only three tuning companies intervened on the Seicento to create the "mean" versions that were destined almost exclusively for racing. Giannini built the 73 HP 600 cc Sport GTO that reached 106 miles per hour (170 kph); the German company G-Tech built the 114 HP Evo 2 Turbo that reached 127 miles per hour (204 kph); and Novitech, which was also German, built a 99 HP Seicento.

122 VINTAGE COLORS (LIGHT BLUE, CREAM, SAGE GREEN, AND LIGHT GRAY BLUE) AND THE TWO MOUSTACHE WINGS BESIDE THE LOGO CHARACTERIZED THE ANNIVERSARY EDITION.

122-123 THE 600 50TH ANNIVERSARY HAD HUBCAPS THAT MATCHED THE BODY COLOR AND A STRIPE THAT RAN ALONG THE HOOD, ROOF, AND HATCHBACK. BOTH FEATURES WERE REMINISCENT OF THE 1950S.

BACK TO THE NUMBERS: THE 600 III SERIES AND 50TH ANNIVERSARY (2005-2008)

The birth of a brand: the 500, from the 2007 model on

In the first years of the new millennium, Fiat was at the end of one of its most difficult periods, marked by the auto-industry crisis in 2001 and by the death of Gianni Agnelli in 2003. In 2000, the company signed a financial and industrial agreement with the American company General Motors, which led to its first shared projects, one of which was the Alfa Romeo 159. In 2004, the new managing director, Sergio Marchionne, decided to make a radical change, and in May 2005, in a move that was financially advantageous for Fiat, he broke the agreement with GM and set out on a path that would lead to the foundation of Fiat-Chrysler Automobiles. The launch of new models was preceded by a great brand-image campaign that focused on company affection and history. The Fiat clothing line, conceived by Lapo Elkann, who had come to the company in 2002 as

communications director, came out in the same period. Sweatshirts with the vintage logo, produced in Padua by Hydrogen, were an immediate success, even with VIPs and clients who drove supercars every day. It was the prelude to the launch of the 500 that would come out in 2007 as a high-end city car. Once again, the 500 had invented a new market sector—and, once again, it was destined to succeed. In the following years, the name was associated with a line of products that were different from those of the Fiat brand, and that included models like the 500 L and 500 X, which became part of a sector that had nothing to do with city cars. The hypothesis of making the 500 a brand of its own arose more than once, and it seemed to gain ground with the 2020 fully electric Nuova 500, which has the Fiat brand on its trunk and its wheel hubs but not on its front end.

124-125 THE SHAPE OF THE 500 USA 1957 EDITION (2015) COMPARED TO THAT OF THE 500D (1960). ALTHOUGH THEIR SIZES ARE COMPLETELY DIFFERENT, THE ASPECT AND THE PROPORTIONS OF THE 2007 MODEL REMAINED TRUE TO THOSE OF ITS FORERUNNER.

A PREVIEW OF THE 500: TREPIÙNO (2004)

It was initially called the Trepiùno. It was never destined for production; it was a show car, conceived to demonstrate Fiat's future design choices—and it went straight to the heart, just as intended. The press at the Geneva Motor Show in 2004 seemed to report on nothing other than its lines, which perfectly recreated the 500 produced between 1957 and 1975. They even forgot to mention the revolutionary seat layout that gave the vehicle its name of "three plus one," the three being two comfortable seats in front and one behind the front passenger's seat, and the one a fourth makeshift seat behind the driver in case of an emergency. The headlines of the trade fair's newspaper read "Welcome back, 500" and elicited a comparison that Fiat did not dare to: the comparison to its iconic ancestor. The major news sources had more to say about the prototype than about Italy's supercars. The Trepiùno was not a result of a market analysis and almost shamelessly recalled its precursor, even more so than Volkswagen's New Beetle had done. At the time, Roberto Giolito was director of Advanced Design, a department that was separate from the Centro Stile Fiat and studied the brand's DNA rather than automotive megatrends. He reported that "in 2001, we put together a group of interns and young project designers, not just engineers but people with degrees in

communications, architects, and materials experts. (. . .) We analyzed the 8V and other Fiat vehicles that were famous for their innovative prototype, like the 600 Multipla, the 127 and the Uno. (. . .) Because Italian design means attention to how something is produced, a detail in craftsmanship, but also open-minded innovation with regard to materials. Italian industrial designers created objects such as the Olivetti Valentine typewriter by Sottsass and King, Brionvega's Algol television by Sapper and Zanuso, Olivetti's Divisumma calculator by Bellini. . . ." When they returned from Geneva, Giolito and his team embarked on a mission: to mass-produce that vehicle, in synergy with what would become the group's new "minimals": the new Panda and the Series III Lancia Y. At that point, it was clear that the car would be called the 500. It would be functional and "minimal-chic" but not poor, with interior noise control and precision pressing and assembling that would accompany the vehicle from its prototype to its mass-produced series. It would be produced at the Polish plant, Tychy, which was soon due to halt production of the Seicento. During the design phase, a web campaign called "500 wants you" brought more than 280,000 visitors to interact with planners with their suggestions and needs.

126 THE TREPIÙNO (WHITE, LEFT) WITH TAILLIGHTS THAT WOULD BE REPLACED WITH VERTICAL ONES, AND AN INTERMEDIATE MODEL WITH AN ALREADY REVISED WHEELBASE; IT STILL HAD THE ROUND BLUE BADGE LAUNCHED IN 1999.

127 THE DEFINITIVE 500 IN A SERIES OF SKETCHES THAT HIGHLIGHT THE STYLE ELEMENTS DERIVED FROM THE 1957 "MODELLO 110." THE LOGO HERE IS STILL THE FIAT 100TH ANNIVERSARY VERSION.

THE FIRST GENERATION: STANDARD SERIES, ONE-OFFS, AND LIMITED EDITIONS (2007)

On March 5, 2006, Fiat announced its "500 days to the 500"; and on July 4 of the following year, exactly fifty years after the launch of its inspiring muse, the 500 of the 21st century was revealed. The city of Turin stopped once again, this time to watch the presentation as it was broadcast live to the nation. The splendor of the event rivaled the Olympic Games ceremonies of the previous year. The 500s were parked in Piazza Vittorio Veneto, under car covers that reproduced the image of the 1957 model. At the end of the ceremony, in front of the authorities, the press, and an audience selected from owners of the historical model, 150 500s were presented to the public. The look was almost exactly that of the Trepiùno. The total length of the car was increased to 139 inches (3550 mm) to facilitate the traditional seating layout of two in the front and two in the back. The small, vintage-style dashboard had analogic and digital instruments and a band that matched the body color, reminiscent of the first 500. Air vents, the radio, and the power-window switches were at the center of the panel. There was no room for an infotainment system, and the optional periscope-style GPS device was mounted on the dashboard. The 500 debuted in TV advertisements with Sergio Marchionne's short movie "Manifesto," in which he narrated moments of Italian history with portraits of Giovanni Falcone and Paolo Borsellino, magistrates killed by the Mafia, and of Pope John Paul II. The images were accompanied by the words of the writer Massimo Gramellini read by the actor Ricky Tognazzi, and the music of Sergio Allevi. The ad ended with "Fiat belongs to all of you."

On July 10 of the same year, a new model was presented to the public in thirty squares throughout Italy. The engines used initially were the Fire 1,200 cc with two valves per cylinder that delivered 69 HP and had a maximum speed of 105 mph (169 kph)(from 2008, it was also available with stop-start technology), a 100 HP Fire 1,400 cc with a maximum speed of 113 mph (182 kph), and a 75 HP diesel Multijet 1,300 cc with a maximum speed of 102 mph (165 kph). It was offered in three trim versions: Pop, which was the simplest; Lounge; and Sport. The last two were priced identically and were more complete; standard equipment on the Lounge included a panoramic glass roof, while the Sport had a more racecar feel. The car debuted in Brazil in 2009, where it was sold until the middle of the following decade.

128-129 THE MULTI-FUNCTION STEERING WHEEL WAS WHITE ON 500S THAT HAD A LIGHT COLORED DASHBOARD AND BLACK ON THOSE WITH A DARK ONE. ON THE BOTTOM, A 500 DECORATED WITH A SERIES OF STICKERS.

SQUEEZE

Put some zing into spring with the new Fiat 500, and you'll end up with a smile as wide as that front grille. The chic-ly designed, cheekily angled headlights will show you the way. Want to let the music play? Stream your favourite tunes through handsfree Bluetooth, and stay connected to your social networks with the 5" touchscreen Uconnect® Radio Live*. Let the juice loose!

FRESH 500

fiat.co.uk

An LPG-powered version was introduced in 2011. The Pop Star version that followed the Pop had, as standard equipment, air-conditioning and a radio.

In the two years that followed its presentation, the 500 loaded up on awards. It earned the World's Most Beautiful Automobile award, it was the Car of the Year 2008, and it won the Auto Europa 2008, the Auto Trophy, and the Euro Car Body 2007. It was named Best City Car by Top Gear, BBC's very popular series about cars, and it was even nominated as the best compact car in Japan. In 2009, it won the World Design Car of the Year and first prize from the Department of Public Administration and Innovation. In 2011, it took home the Compasso d'Oro Award. When it came to production, however, Fiat was afraid that sales would not equal the car's successful image, which had been stable since the time of the Trepiùno. To saturate the production line, Fiat shared a platform and many components with Ford. The second generation of Ford's small

hatchback, Ka, produced at the Tychy plant on the same line, did not enjoy the same success as the iconic 1996 version. The 500 earned five stars at the Euro NCAP test.

In 2008, the grueling 1958 Liège-Brescia-Liège was reenacted. In the original rally, only 13 of the 36 participating vehicles crossed the finish line, including all of the seven Nuova 500s. The 2,050-mile (3,300 km) itinerary includes a number of alpine passes; from Cortina, cars had to follow the Dolomite chain as far as Ljubljana and then return to Bolzano and on to Brescia through a number of passes. From June 2012 to March 2014, with the Color Therapy program, it was possible to purchase a 500 in one of the program's special colors (Cappuccino Beige, Solo Yellow, Passion Red, Volare Blue, or Carrara Gray), and, after 500 days, exchange it for a 500 in one of the other colors with the same size engine. In 2014, the first change was made: the addition of a TFT 7" monitor to the instrument panel.

130 ADVERTISING FOR THE 500 MADE FOR THE U.K. WITH THE "COLOUR THERAPY" PROGRAM, CUSTOMERS COULD EXCHANGE THEIR 500 FOR ONE OF ANOTHER COLOR AFTER 500 DAYS.

131 THE OPENING UNDER THE BUMPERS MADE IT POSSIBLE TO HIDE THE RADIATOR GRILL AND KEEP THE FRONT END SMOOTH, LIKE THAT OF THE "MODELLO 110."

Before it was put on the market, a special limited edition of 500 cars was produced. It was called the Opening Edition and could be ordered at the Milan Furniture Fair, after having chosen from a wide range of colors and stickers. Included in the 500 Open Editions was one created in collaboration with the designer furniture producer, Cappellini, which had a blue interior and body. One of the two very limited editions that were considered borderline kitsch was the 500 Italia Independent, associated with the Lapo Elkan brand, presented at the Pitti Uomo men's wear show in Florence, with a matte finish and zebra-striped side mirrors. The other was the Pepita, complete with gold finishes and Swarovski crystals. In 2011, the First Edition operation was presented to the Chinese market, where the Mexican-produced 500 had been sold since September. Two celebrities received Special 500s. One was given to the ace soccer player for Juventus, Alessandro del Piero; it was the tenth, in honor of his jersey number. The other went to the television host Piero Chiambretti; it was burgundy, in honor of his favorite soccer team, Turin. The Fender Musical Instrument Corporation, producer of the favorite guitar of many rock stars, decided to dedicate a unique version of its iconic Stratocaster to the 500.

An ambitious event was planned for the launch of the 500—a trip from Turin to Beijing, following the route of the legendary 1907 Beijing-Paris Rally that was won by the Itala 35/45 HP with Luigi Barzini, Scipione Borghese, and Ettore Guizzardi onboard. The caravan was made up of the hundred-year-old Itala that had already retraced the route from Beijing to Europe in 1989, and the classic Iveco 330.30 ANW trucks that were used in the first Overland expeditions, led by Beppe Tenti. The caravan left Turin on July 11 and reached Beijing on September 20. The diesel-engine 500 Overland was painted orange, the official color of the expedition; today it is on display at the Fiat Heritage Hub in Turin.

132-133 THE POP WITH A 1,200 CC ENGINE WAS AVAILABLE FOR THE EUROPEAN MARKETS IN A SPECIAL BUT NOT LIMITED TWO-TONED RED-AND-WHITE EDITION. IN JAPAN, THE EDITION WAS LIMITED TO 50 UNITS.

THE HEROINE OF TWO WORLDS: THE 500 AMERICA (2010–2019)

In April 2009, shortly after Fiat had taken over a minority share of the company in a move that preceded a complete takeover in 2011 and the foundation of FCA in 2014, Chrysler announced that it would distribute the 500 in the United States and presented it in New York. Adapting the 500 for the American market was not a simple task. The model, which Chrysler's Mexican plant in Toluca began manufacturing in 2010, underwent many structural changes compared to the European model, in order to comply with the NHTSA's extremely strict safety regulations. Numerous changes were made to reduce interior noise and to improve the suspension. From the outside, the model was recognizable by the side markers at the extremities of its bumpers; the top version of the Sport range had a special shield on the front bumper. The American 500 was launched at the 2010 Los Angeles Auto Show.

It was powered by a 16-valve 1400 cc engine, also available in a 135 HP version (called Fiat 500 Turbo instead of Abarth in the U.S.), with a 5-speed manual transmission or a 6-speed automatic. It was initially launched in a limited two-toned red-and-white version. April 2013 saw the launch of a special series, the Cattiva, which was two-toned with a shiny black roof available on the Sport and Turbo. The upholstery and dashboard were matte black leather, and body colors included copper, black, red, white, silver, and two special colors: glossy granite and light blue. At the end of the decade, sales of the 500 sedan fell off in the United States, Mexico, and Canada, in part due to the lack of availability in the dealerships, so FCA decided that 2019 would be the last model year of the city car. The 500 L and the 500 X stayed on the market.

134 THE 500 TURBO HAD THE SAME ENGINE AS THE EUROPEAN 500 ABARTH. IN THE U.S., THE ABARTH WAS A PRODUCT LINE, NOT A BRAND, RESERVED TO THE 595 AND 695.

135 THE 500 1957 EDITION WAS BASED ON THE AMERICAN 500 AND PROPOSED THE COLORS AND DETAILS OF THE EUROPEAN 1957 VINTAGE. THE WHEEL ARCHES HAD NOTABLE ORANGE SIDE MARKERS. THE 500 1957 EDITION HAD SEATS UPHOLSTERED IN TOBACCO BROWN LEATHER AND A WHITE DASHBOARD, LIKE THE EUROPEAN VINTAGE 1957.

2008 began with a research prototype, the 500 Aria. It had a start-stop system and an electronic control unit and emitted only 0.35 pounds (98 g) of CO_2 per mile. The Pur-O2 was a standard-equipment version that was developed from the Aria, the first Euro 5 car sold in Italy, actually, ahead of legal standards. In the summer of 2009, the 500 Pur-O2 was dressed up in pink for a series of 50 cars destined for the Italian market, called So Pink. The United Kingdom liked the idea and placed an order, initially for 500 sedans, which were called simply "Pink," and later for 300 cabriolets. The 500,000th 500 came off the line in Tychy in 2010; the half-million mark was reached through sales in 80 countries throughout the world. The Barbie

version was metallic pink with Alcantara laminate in silver and fuchsia, designed to celebrate the 50th birthday of Mattel's iconic doll. Accessories, such as lip-glosses inspired by the world of glamour that matched the car color, followed. A subsequent model, a show car in the same theme, was presented with a kind of runway show through the streets of Milan that ended in front of the Rinascente Department Store in Piazza Duomo. Another version that was inspired by the world of fashion was the 500 Fiorucci Love Therapy (only one was produced), while another one-off version was the 500 Christopher Columbus, created in collaboration with the Numismatic Program of the Department of the Treasury.

136-137 THE SPECIAL VERSION CREATED TO CELEBRATE THE 50TH ANNIVERSARY OF THE BARBIE DOLL WAS PAINTED IN A SPECIAL METALLIC PINK GLITTER EFFECT, WITH CHROME BUMPERS AND A GLASS ROOF.

137 TOP THE PILLARS OF THE BARBIE WERE DECORATED WITH THE FAMOUS MATTEL DOLL'S PROFILE, MADE OF SWAROVSKI CRYSTALS.

137 BOTTOM A MAKEUP KIT THAT CAME WITH THE CAR AND THE 500 LOGO ON THE DASHBOARD, WHICH WAS ALSO MADE WITH SWAROVSKI CRYSTALS.

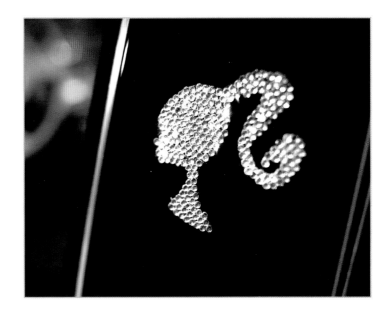

A special but not limited version was the first one dedicated to a fashion brand, Diesel. Beginning in 2008, the jeans manufacturer in Italy's Veneto Region signed a range of four metallic-color versions based on the 500 Sport: dark green, like that of the founder, Renzo Rosso's, personal helicopter; black; brown; and a special pearlescent color, Midnight Indigo. The car was called the Urban Survival Vehicle, a play on the acronym SUV. Its distinguishing features included the air intakes of the classic Fiat 500 under the back window, brushed-steel details, and the interior, which was obviously in denim. The first Diesel 500 C, a cabriolet, was auctioned for charity in May 2009. The version was available in green with a black convertible top, black with a black or red top, and indigo blue with a cream-colored top. A total of ten thousand Diesel 500s were produced. Diabolika, on the other hand, was a very limited edition of only 30 cars, designed in collaboration with Studiotorino. It was matte black with graphics inspired by the Giussani sisters' Diabolik comic books. An additional 30 with one-of-a-kind details were made for the Circleclub circuit, which rents very exclusive vehicles.

138 THE 500 C URBAN SURVIVAL VEHICLE BY DIESEL IN ITS MOST POPULAR COLOR, THE METALLIC GREEN OF THE HELICOPTER BELONGING TO RENZO ROSSO, CREATOR OF THE DIESEL BRAND.

138-139 A TRANSPARENT VIEW OF THE 500 THAT ILLUSTRATES THE "TUTTO AVANTI," FRONT-WHEEL-DRIVE TECHNOLOGY, AND THE REAR AXLE, AS WELL AS THE ROOF STRUCTURE THAT WAS THE SAME FOR THE VERSIONS WITH CLOSED ROOFS AND MOON ROOFS.

140 DIABOLIKA WAS A LIMITED SERIES OF 30 MATTE BLACK UNITS. CONCEIVED BY STUDIOTORINO, IT WAS DEDICATED TO THE FANS OF DIABOLIK, THE SERIES OF DETECTIVE COMICS CREATED BY THE GIUSSANI SISTERS.

140-141 THE BACK RESTS OF THE FRONT SEATS WERE DECORATED WITH CLOSE-UPS OF DIABOLIK AND HIS COMPANION, EVA KANT. THE INTERIOR UPHOLSTERY AND MATERIALS WERE COMPLETELY BLACK.

THE STARS AS A ROOF: 500 C I SERIES (2009-2015)

The 500 C (the C stands for cabriolet) was presented at the Geneva Motor Show in 2009. It reintroduced the concept of the 1957 Nuova 500, with a fabric sunroof that opened all the way to the trunk while keeping its pillars and doorframes. The electrically powered top and its glass rear window fold down into the parcel shelf so the car's trunk space is almost the same as that of the sedan, 6.4 cubic feet (182 l) instead of 6.5 cubic feet (185 l). The Lounge was originally the basic version, sold alongside the sportier Rock with low-profile tires. The following year, a simpler and more economical version, the Pop, completed the series.

142 THE 500C WITH ITS TOP UP. IT WAS INITIALLY PROPOSED WITH THE SAME TRIM PACKAGE AS THAT OF THE TOP VERSIONS OF THE SEDAN. THE LESS-EXPENSIVE POP CAME OUT LATER.

143 A VIEW OF THE APEX OF THE TOP AS IT OPENS. SINCE THE TOP DID NOT FOLD DOWN INTO THE TRUNK, THE TRUNK RETAINED THE SAME CAPACITY AS THAT OF THE SEDAN.

144 THE LOGO ON THE TRUNK OF THE TWINAIR VERSION OF THE 500 I SERIES (TOP). ON THE BOTTOM, THE 900 CC TWIN CYLINDER, WHICH WAS CHARACTERIZED BY ITS HIGH SPECIFIC POWER.

144-145 THE PERFORMANCE OF THE TWINAIRS IN THE INITIAL VERSIONS WAS HIGHLIGHTED WITH DARK-COLORED SPORTY DETAILS. THE FRONT GRILL WAS WIDER THAN THAT OF THE FOUR-CYLINDER.

BACK TO THE TWIN-CYLINDER: THE 500 TWINAIR I SERIES (2011-2015)

Geneva 2011 was the stage for the debut of the Twinair, which had been announced in October of the previous year. The small, high-performance 900 cc turbo, initially an 85 HP, pushed the 500 to 107 miles per hour (173 kph). The spokesperson for the launch was the Formula 1 driver Fernando Alonso, who was part of the Ferrari team at the time. In 2012, the sporty characteristics of the little twin-cylinder were emphasized with an esthetic trim kit from Abarth that had black alloy wheels, sporting seats, racing pedals, side skirts, rear spoilers, and special decals to pair with the body colors, red and black.

146-147 PRESENTATION IN THE U.S. OF THE 500 E MADE FOR THE CALIFORNIA MARKET. THE CAR WAS PRECEDED BY A CONCEPT CAR, THE 500 ELETTRA BEV (BATTERY ELECTRIC VEHICLE), WHICH WAS ALMOST DEFINITIVE.

147 THE ELECTRICAL OUTLET FOR RECHARGING THE BATTERIES OF THE AMERICAN 500 E, LOCATED BEHIND THE FUEL DOOR.

THE JOLT THAT CAME FROM AMERICA: THE 500E (2012-2019)

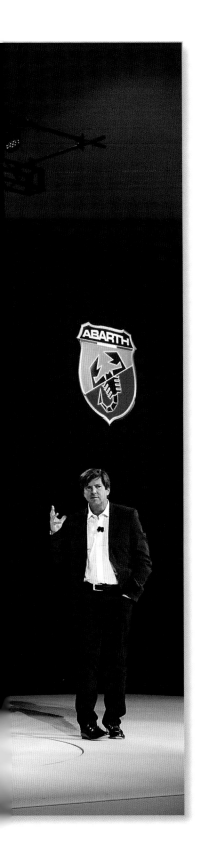

The vehicle that stood out at the Chrysler stand at the 2010 North American Auto Show in Detroit was the 500 Elettra BEV (Battery Electric Vehicle), a research prototype powered by the American company and later presented at the Bologna Motor Show. It was the Hybrid Tech prototype that put a hybrid driveline under the hood of a 500 for the first time, with an electric motor, Twinair engines, and an automated dual-clutch transmission. The definitive version of the 500e came out in the U.S. at the end of 2012. The first series of 150 cars was destined for California. Some arrived in Europe as well. In Turin, they became part of the car-sharing circuit Io Guido, and they were used as service vehicles at the Milan Expo in 2015. Some 500e's arrived in Norway, sold by an independent dealer without permission from Fiat.

148-149 SOME AMERICAN 500 ES WERE OFFICIALLY IMPORTED TO ITALY AND GERMANY TO BE USED EXPERIMENTALLY IN CAR-SHARING NETWORKS; THIS ONE IS GERMAN.

149 TOP THE RECHARGING OUTLET, MOVED TO THE FRONT OF THE CAR UNDER THE FIAT LOGO.

149 BOTTOM THE CHARGE-STATUS INDICATOR LIGHT ON THE INTERACTIVE DISPLAY AND THE 500 E LOGO.

The first 500 Gucci was introduced at the 2011 Geneva Motor Show. It was created by the Centro Stile Fiat in collaboration with the creative director of the Florentine fashion house, Frida Giannini. It was available in white or glossy black. It had a stripe in the classic Gucci colors (two dark green bands with a red band between them) along the side of the body, under the windows, and in the middle of the seats and seatbacks, which were black with light gray sides, and the legendary Gucci signature on the trunk. At the same time, a line of accessories inspired by the 500 was sold in Gucci boutiques. The model produced for the U.S., the 2013 Gucci II, was available with a trim package called Interno Notte, or night interior, with black seats and dashboard and the Gucci stripe. The same details of the sedan were offered in the 500 C, which also had a Gucci stripe on its fabric sunroof. An app was specifically developed that allowed clients to design and order their 500s. The 500 La Petite Robe Noire was available only on the French market. It took its name from a Guerlain perfume. 250 were produced based on the 500 sedan with a panoramic glass sunroof, and 250 were made from the 500 C. It was available in black or white, with two-toned, Poltrona Frau Leather seats and fashion accessories that included a clothes hook on the seatback. It was powered by the 69 HP Fire 1,200 cc and the 85 and 105 HP Twinair engines.

150 THE 500 GUCCI SEDAN VERSION. GLOSSY BLACK WAS ONE OF THE AVAILABLE COLORS. THE LOGO OF THE FASHION HOUSE APPEARED ON THE CENTRAL PILLAR AND ON THE TRUNK.

151 A 500 C GUCCI IN WHITE, THE OTHER AVAILABLE COLOR. THE TOP WAS DARK FOR THE WHITE VERSION ALSO, AND HAD A RED-GREEN-RED GUCCI STRIPE IN THE MIDDLE.

UNIQUE AND SPECIAL: THE LAST LIMITED EDITIONS OF THE FIRST SERIES (2013-2015)

The rollout of the 500 America in the United States was celebrated a bit late, in May of 2012, with a special edition of 500 numbered vehicles created in collaboration with the popstar Jennifer Lopez. The cars, which were destined for the European market, were painted a special dark blue and had mirror covers with a stars-and-stripes pattern. FCA used its Twitter account to assign the first car of the series. The more aggressive-looking 500 Street came out in June 2012. The end of the same year saw the launch of the 500 S, a Pop with a spoiler, side-skirts, a redesigned valance panel, 15" wheels, tinted windows, a matte gray dashboard, and gray chrome details. It was available in nine colors, and sports upholstery was standard equipment. Customers who ordered through Facebook could have the Dualogic automatic transmission for the same price as the manual transmission. A few modifications to the S gave birth to the Street, which looked similar to the European version of the same name. Shortly afterward, in April 2013, the millionth 500 produced in Europe rolled off the line at Tychy.

152 THE 500 AMERICA WAS A SPECIAL 2012 SERIES MADE FOR THE EUROPEAN MARKET TO CELEBRATE THE LAUNCH OF THE 500 IN THE U.S.A.

152-153 THE REARVIEW MIRROR OF THE 500 AMERICA. COLORS AND DECORATIONS WERE DEVELOPED IN COLLABORATION WITH THE POP STAR JENNIFER LOPEZ.

154

In March 2011, the coachbuilder Zagato presented a coupe version of the 500. It had a sloping rear roofline and raised back windows that produced two triangles in the C pillar, as well as Zagato's signature "double bubble" in the roof, a feature that the coachbuilder used in many of his creations of the 1950s and 60s. After an initial announcement that the car would be produced in series, the project was abandoned and the dark yellow metallic coupe, powered by a 105 HP Twinair, was the only one of its kind. In 2015, the 500 Playa was announced for the European market. A beach cruiser, much like the Ghia Jolly, it was produced by the Turin coachbuilder Vernagallo, who had built and homologated the 500 Mare, a beach car built on the historical 500s that were already in circulation. But there was no follow-through on the project, and the only homologated Playa was sold at an auction to a collector.

Eight years after its launch, the career of the first series of 500s drew to a close with two special series proposed in colors that would make them easily recognizable. In April, the 500 and 500 C Vintage '57 were rolled out in a palette of 12 colors that reintroduced those of the first series of the Nuova 500. Engine choices included the 69 HP Fire 1,200 cc and the 65, 85, or 105 HP Twinair 900 cc. The Cult, which came out in May, was available in a very pale shade of mint green (the most requested), white, and blue Italy, in both coupe and cabriolet versions, powered by a 105 HP Twinair. The interior was available in black, red, or tobacco brown leather and special finish chrome accents. Paolo Sorrentino, who had just come back from his win at the Academy Awards with his movie "The Great Beauty," participated in the presentation.

154-155 THE VINTAGE 1957, IN SOFT COLORS INSPIRED BY THE PALETTE OF THE NUOVA 500, WITH A WHITE ROOF, LEATHER UPHOLSTERY, AND SPECIAL HUBCAPS; IT WAS ONE OF THE LAST SPECIAL EDITIONS OF THE FIRST SERIES.

156-157 TOP THE CULT HAD EXQUISITE INTERIOR DETAILS WITH LEATHER UPHOLSTERY AND STEERING WHEEL. THE NEW DIGITAL DASHBOARD AND THE 105 HP TWINAIR ENGINE DEBUTED WITH THIS MODEL.

156-157 BOTTOM OF THE THREE COLORS AVAILABLE FOR THE CULT, THE LIGHT GREEN LATTEMENTA WAS CERTAINLY THE MOST POPULAR. THE PRICE OF THE SEDAN WAS THE SAME AS THAT OF THE 500 C.

AN ICON REINVENTED: THE 500 II SERIES (SINCE 2015)

158-159 THE MOST EVIDENT CHANGE IN THE BACK OF THE CAR WERE ITS PARKING LIGHTS, WHERE AN INSERT THAT MATCHED THE COLOR OF THE CAR BODY HAD BEEN ADDED. IN THE PHOTO, THE TOP OF THE LINE 500 C STAR.

159 THE RESTYLING THAT LED TO THE SECOND SERIES WAS FOCUSED ON DETAILS SUCH AS PARKING LIGHTS. THE ROCKSTAR VERSION WAS PROPOSED IN THE SAME MATTE COLOR AS THE MATT BLACK S.

The second series of the European 500 debuted in 2015. It was presented on July 4, as usual. It had the benefit of the many structural improvements that had been made to the American version; and, although small esthetic details were changed, its vintage approach and inspiration were the same. Lighting groups were modified, particularly the taillights, which had been changed to LED lights and had a central insert that matched the body color. The front end was redesigned; and the choice of engines included, obviously, the 900 cc Twinair Turbo in two rather spirited versions (85 and 105 HP) and the more tranquil 95 HP 1,200 cc in-line four-cylinder, which was also available in a bi-fuel gasoline/methane version. The only diesel engine offered was the 95 HP 1,300 cc Multijet. The Pop, Sport, and Lounge remained on the market. In November 2019, a 500 was the 12 millionth vehicle produced in Tychy. In November, a new diesel engine, the 95 HP Multijet II, debuted. Shortly before the launch, Bottega Conticelli, a luxury leather artisan, customized a special 500 C with leather and fine wood details; it was donated to the Robert F. Kennedy Human Rights Organization, which auctioned it for charity.

The fierce look of the S was proposed again for the second series. Both the sedan and the 500 C were available in two matte colors, blue and green. Its specially designed bumper made it distinguishable from the normal versions. Frau Leather upholstery was available on request.

INSPIRED BY THE SEA: THE 500 RIVA AND DOLCEVITA (2016–2017)

In 2016, when the 500 Riva was created in collaboration with the Sarnico-based boat maker, producer of some of the most sophisticated powerboats in the world, it was launched as the "smallest yacht in the world." It was built on the 500 sedan and the 500 C and was available in a special version, painted an exclusive metallic blue with a green-and-white stripe that underlined the beltline. The dashboard was in mahogany wood, which, together with the white leather seats, evoked the typical tones of Riva yachts. Five hundred sedans and five hundred 500 Cs were produced. Fifty of the 500 Cs were proposed in an even more special version, the Tender to Paris, with a Beats audio system, the same used in the limited edition of the 500 L in 2014. When Riva production was over, another marine-inspired 500 was rolled out. The Dolcevita was the 20th limited edition of the 500 in 12 years of production. The sedan had a panoramic glass roof, and the fabric top of the cabriolet was lined with beach umbrella stripes, reminiscent of the 500 C that was celebrating its 10th birthday. The body was white with a double red stripe.

160   THE DASHBOARD OF THE 500 RIVA IN MAHOGANY, THE SAME WOOD USED TO MAKE RIVA POWERBOATS IN SARNICO.

160-161   THE SAME DETAILS OF THE SEDAN WERE FEATURED IN THE 500 C RIVA; THE TOP WAS DARK BLUE.

162 AND 163 THE DOLCEVITA WAS INSPIRED BY THE LIGHT COLORS OF SUMMER. IT WAS PRODUCED AS A SEDAN WITH A NON-OPENABLE MOON ROOF, AND AS A 500C WITH A BLUE-AND-WHITE-STRIPED TOP.

OFF TO THE BEACH: 500C SPIAGGINA '58 (2018)

The 60th birthday of the Jolly Ghia was celebrated with the launch of the 500 C Spiaggina '58. Inspired by the first 500s and created in the wake of what had been the Vintage 1957 and parallel to the 1957 American Edition, it was produced in a limited series of 1958 cars. The blue-and-white-striped top brought to mind the fabric of beach umbrellas and lounge chairs and the surrey top of the Jolly. The body was painted blue, and the design of the alloy wheels resembled the steel wheels of the 500 D and F. The interior was in nautical colors with horizontal blue and white stripes. The creative hub founded in Milan by Lapo Elkann, Garage Italia Custom, created a number of one-of-a-kind custom Spiaggina '58s. One of these was designed in collaboration with Pininfarina. It was completely open; the only thing jutting from above the beltline was a roll bar, which served structural and safety purposes. In the place of rear seating was an open trunk area with wooden slats that the designer said could be outfitted with a shower.

164-165 ANOTHER NAUTICALLY INSPIRED MODEL WAS THE SPIAGGINA '58; 1,958 UNITS WERE PRODUCED ON THE BASE OF THE 500 C. THE MODEL WAS PAINTED VOLARE BLUE WITH A FINE WHITE STRIPE ALONG THE BELTLINE. IT HAD A STRIPED TOP, AND ITS WHEEL RIMS WERE REMINISCENT OF THOSE ON THE EUROPEAN VINTAGE 1957 (BASED ON THE FIRST SERIES) AND ON THE 1957 AMERICAN EDITION.

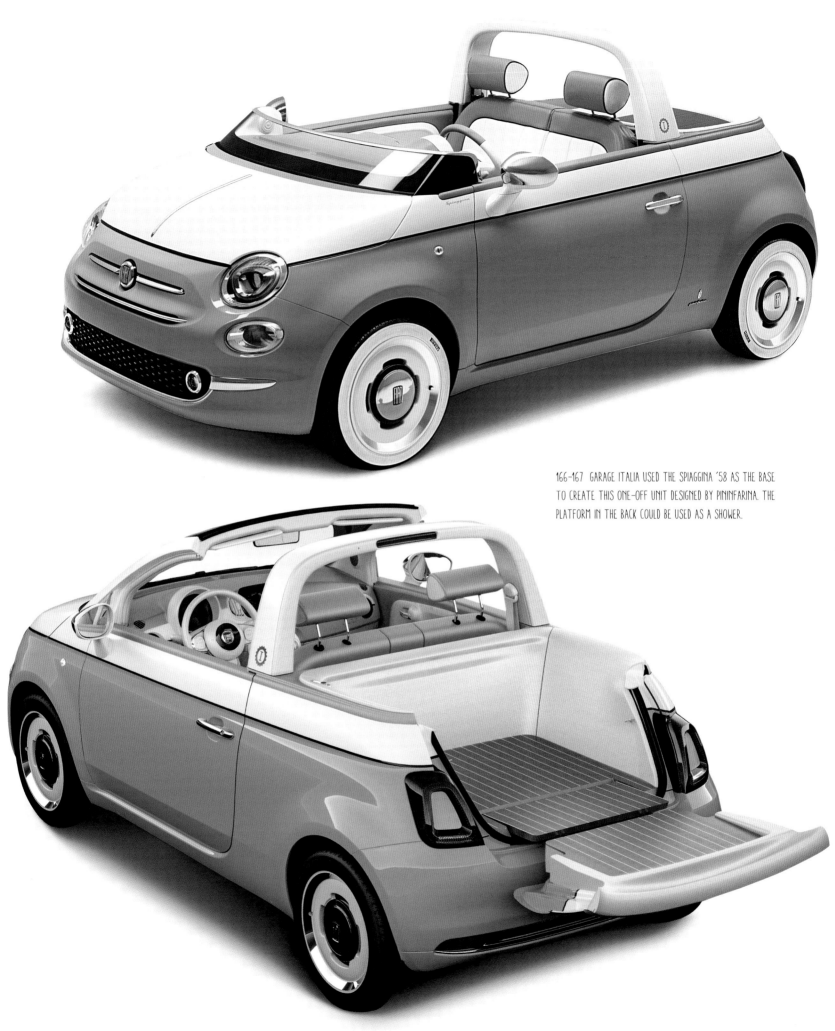

166-167 GARAGE ITALIA USED THE SPIAGGINA '58 AS THE BASE TO CREATE THIS ONE-OFF UNIT DESIGNED BY PININFARINA. THE PLATFORM IN THE BACK COULD BE USED AS A SHOWER.

ELEGANCE IN BURGUNDY: 500 COLLEZIONE AND BY REPETTO (2018)

168 THIS COMBINATION OF CARRARA GRAY AND OPERA BURGUNDY (CALLED THE "BRUNELLO TWO-TONE") WAS FEATURED IN THE 500 COLLEZIONE. IT WAS CONCEIVED FOR THE 2018 FALL/WINTER SEASON IN COLLABORATION WITH THE MAGAZINE *L'UOMO VOGUE*.

168-169 THIS BURGUNDY GLASS-ROOFED EDITION WAS CREATED FOR THE FRENCH MARKET. IT WAS CONCEIVED IN COLLABORATION WITH THE PARIS FASHION HOUSE REPETTO, FAMOUS FOR ITS BALLET WEAR.

Three special 500 Cs called Collezione were created in 2018. The first of the series came out in May, the Primavera, which was available in white and aqua blue, white and gray, and white and green. Later, the Fall/Winter version was presented. It came in white and gray or in Opera Burgundy and Carrara Gray, with a dark gray pinstriped interior. The Fall/Winter Collezione was also available in solid colors: Cortina Gray, Carrara Gray, Vesuvius Black, and Opera Burgundy. A two-toned Opera Burgundy and Carrara Gray version called "Brunello," with luxury interior, was created in collaboration with the magazine "L'Uomo Vogue." An all-burgundy special version with ivory stripes and a Frau Leather interior was created for the French market, in collaboration with the Paris fashion house Repetto, famous for its ballet wear. Presented in November 2018, it was built on the base of the sedan with a Skydome glass roof and was available with a 69 HP Fire 1,200 cc or an 85 HP Twinair 90. Buyers also received a pair of ballet shoes, a personalized key holder, and a small vial of Repetto perfume.

FIAT'S FIRST HYBRID: THE 500 HYBRID (2020)

Hybrid technology made it under the hood of the 500 at the beginning of 2020. This mild hybrid had a 3.6 kW motor generator that served as starter and alternator as well as providing additional torque to the traction engine (a three-cylinder 70 HP Firefly aspirated engine) during transients. During braking, it worked as an alternator and recharged a Samsung SDI lithium battery that powered the motor alternator when torque was required. The reduction in transients allowed for fuel (and emissions) savings of about 20%. Its maximum speed was 103 miles per hour (167 kph) and it had a manual 6-speed transmission. The arrival of the hybrid was celebrated with the Hybrid Launch Edition, in dew green with a black or gray sunroof for the 500 C, special wheels, and the logo on the pillar.

170-171 THE LAUNCH VERSION OF THE HYBRID 500 WAS DEVELOPED ON THE BODY OF THE SECOND SERIES; IT WAS AVAILABLE IN DEW GREEN. THE TOP OF THE 500 C COULD BE GRAY OR BLACK.

171 THE HYBRID 500 WAS POWERED BY THE NEW 70 HP THREE-CYLINDER FIREFLY ENGINE, WITH AN INTEGRATED 3.6 KW ELECTRIC MOTOR-GENERATOR.

GOODBYE, GASOLINE: THE NUOVA 500 (2020)

The new electric 500 was created with a completely new platform, different from that of the American and European versions with heat engines, while the exterior restyling was minimal. It was the first full-electric vehicle of the FCA range and the only 500 of its generation to be produced in Italy, at the Mirafiori plant in Turin. It was baptized with a name reminiscent of the iconic model 110, Nuova 500, with no reference to its electric motor. The Nuova 500 also served as the base for three one-of-a-kind cars, created by three Italian luxury brands: Giorgio Armani (500 Giorgio Armani), Bulgari (B.500 Mai Troppo), and Kartell (500 Kartell). The models were painted with a particular technique that creates a three dimensional, fabric-like finish in colors strongly associated with each brand, Graygreen, Saffron, and Blu Kartell, and had precious details like Armani's full-grain leather seats and Bulgari's gold and diamonds. Its 87 kW motor can take the car to a maximum speed of 93 miles per hour (150 kph) (automatically limited), while its 42 kWh battery pack guarantees a range of 199 miles (320 km) and recharges to 85% in 30 minutes thanks to its rapid-charge system. The Easy Wallbox, developed by Engie EPS, needs no installation and makes it possible to recharge the car's battery pack on a standard domestic electricity grid. The car's selector allows drivers to choose from three driving modes: Sherpa, Range, and Normal. The most energy-thrifty is Sherpa; and in the intermediate mode, Range, drivers use only the accelerator; the deceleration of the motor stops the car. The car's automated safety system makes it a level 2 self-driving vehicle. Its fifth-generation Uconnect infotainment system offers a complete connection and supports integration with Apple and Android smartphones. That the Fiat logo is no longer on the front of the car underlines the 500's identity as a brand of its own. The logo still appears on the back of the car and on the wheel hubs. The front end is more vertical, and the elliptical-shaped headlights make an "eyebrow" on the hood. The wheels are bigger, and the wheelbase is 0.8 inches (20 mm) longer. The interior upholstery is made with eco-friendly fibers such as faux leather and Seaqual, a fabric made from recycled plastic collected from the sea.

172-173 ITS HEADLIGHTS, DOOR HANDLES, AND FRONT END WERE ALL REVISED WITH RESPECT TO THE HEAT-ENGINE VERSION, WHICH DID NOT UNDERGO THE RESTYLING. THERE IS NO FIAT LOGO ON THE FRONT END.

THE SCORPION IS BACK: ABARTH 500 (2008) AND ABARTH 500 CABRIO (2010)

174-175 THE ABARTHS BASED ON THE 500 C BODY, BORN IN 2010, WERE BAPTIZED 500 CABRIO AND WERE IMMEDIATELY AVAILABLE IN A RANGE OF TWO-TONE COLOR COMBINATIONS.

175 THE GERMAN TUNER KARL SCHNORR CREATED THE FIRST RACING-STYLE 500 ABARTH BEFORE THE OFFICIAL VERSIONS OF THE MORE POWERFUL MODELS LIKE THE 595 AND 695 CAME OUT.

In March 2008, Abarth left its old location in Corso Marche (which it had abandoned in the '80s and then briefly took back as a dealership that was an investee company of Fiat called Officine Abarth) to move to Officina 83 in Fiat's Mirafiori plant. To celebrate the occasion, it launched its first 500, in line with Carlo Abarth's original philosophy, according to which a car must go "to the race track on Sunday and the office on Monday." Power was provided by a 135 HP 1,400-cc turbo engine with variable mapping. In Normal mode, peak torque reached 180 Nm at 2,000 rpm, and in Sport it reached 206 Nm at 3,000 rpm. Its electronic distributor favored the delivery of torque to the wheel with more adhesion. It was available with a manual transmission or an automatic transmission with a paddle shifter. Its special braking system had oversized Brembo discs that were front-axle ventilated. Beginning in 2013, this version was renamed the 500 Custom. In November, a souped-up version came out (160 HP, 230 Nm of torque, drilled, ventilated disc brakes, Eibach springs) with historical name Esseesse. The Esseesse kit and the Esseesse Koni kit, which was identical except for the Koni shock absorbers with selective damping, were also available for cars that were already in circulation. In addition to the street version, the project included the Assetto Corsa, a non-homologated racing version that was destined for racing pilots in a single-brand championship. It weighed 2,050 pounds (930 kg), 396 less than the series version, and had a 190 HP engine and a roll bar. The transmission was the manual 6-speed used in the Punto Evo Abarth.

In 2010, the European Abarth versions also became available on the 500 C body, with the name 500 Cabrio (and later, 595 Cabrio and 695 Cabrio). On the 150th anniversary of Italy's unification in 2011, the 500 Abarth celebrated with 150 numbered units of the 500 C Esseesse Cabrio Italia, in Abu Dhabi blue with a black top. It had leather Sabelt seats, GPS with a telemetry function, and 17'' wheels. The launch included a vast series of two-toned combinations that were reserved for the version with the same name.

16"

17"

ABARTH

17"

176-177 THE ALLOY WHEELS AVAILABLE FOR THE TWO-TONED EDITION OF THE
500 CABRIO ABARTH. THE 15-INCH WHEELS HAD EIGHT SPOKES; THE 16-INCH
WHEELS HAD FIVE. ALL VERSIONS HAD LARGER BRAKE DISCS AND RED BRAKE
CALIPERS.

177 TOP THE DASHBOARD OF THE VERSIONS WITH A SEMI-AUTOMATIC
TRANSMISSION THAT FUNCTIONED WITH A GEARSHIFT OR PADDLES. THE
SPORTING-STYLE PEDALS WERE IN ALUMINUM.

177 BOTTOM THE CABRIO ITALIA, A SERIES OF 150 UNITS LAUNCHED IN
2011 TO CELEBRATE THE 150TH ANNIVERSARY OF ITALY'S UNIFICATION, HAD
LEATHER-UPHOLSTERED SABELT SEATS. THE BODY WAS PAINTED THE METALLIC
DARK BLUE SEEN ON THE DASHBOARD.

VERY FAST AND SPECIAL:
THE LIMITED SERIES OF THE 500 ABARTH (2008)

Sales of the little Abarth began with a special version to underline its future as a collector's item. Named the Opening Edition, it had leather seats and a Blue & Me infotainment system, and was available in white or Campo Volo gray, with the option of a red-and-white-checkered roof. A total of 149 units were produced, 100 of which were for the Italian market. Also from 2008 was the Da Zero a Cento series that commemorated the 100th anniversary of Carlo Abarth's birth. It derived from the Esseesse with an exhaust system called Record Monza, a name that reminds one of another glorious page in the history of Abarth. It was Nuvolari gray with tone-on-tone decals and chrome mirrors. Its short gear ratio made it possible to reach 62 miles per hour (100 kph) in 7.2 seconds. The 2009 special edition, Tributo Ferrari, was a preview of the 695, the model that would be presented in 2014. It was the second vehicle in the world to have both the Abarth and Ferrari trademarks, after a one-off in 1953, the Abarth/Ferrari 166/250 Mille Miglia. It was powered by a 180 HP 1,400 turbo-cc T-jet engine with an automatic transmission and paddle shifter on the steering column, Sabelt racing seats, Jaeger instruments like those of the Ferrari, aluminum plates in place of mats, aluminum pedals, Brembo four-piston brake calipers, and a special Record Monza exhaust system. 1,199 were made in Corsa red, 299 in Modena Yellow, 99 in Titanio gray, and 99 in Abu Dhabi blue.

178-179 IN 2009, THE 695 TRIBUTO FERRARI PRECEDED THE ROLLOUT OF THE MORE POWERFUL 695 IN 2012. IT WAS ONLY THE SECOND CAR IN HISTORY TO BEAR BOTH THE FERRARI AND ABARTH BRANDS. THE 1,696 UNITS PRODUCED WERE AVAILABLE IN RED, YELLOW, GRAY, AND BLUE AND HAD THE SAME JAEGER DASHBOARD INSTRUMENTS AS THE FERRARI.

THE FIRST SOUPED-UP VERSION: ABARTH 595 (2011)

The 2011 Bologna Motor Show was the stage for the launch of the Abarth 595, the series between the 500 and the 695, reminiscent of the Abarth of the '60s. The 595 Custom had a 140 HP turbo engine with 260 Nm of torque in Normal mode and 260 in Sport mode. Sale of the Custom Trofeo, a limited special edition of 250 units produced exclusively for the U.K. market, began in October; it had 17" rims and came in gray, black, and red. The interior was leather and Alutex, an aluminum glass fiber material. There were also three ready-to-drive, high performance versions in the group. The Turismo was launched in a two-toned gray and red limited series with a 160 HP engine, self-ventilating front brakes, and Koni shock absorbers. The difference between the Competizione and the Turismo was the Competizione's Record Monza

exhaust system and some esthetic features such as its accents in gray satin rather than chrome, Xenon headlights, and side decals. A 595 tuning kit was available to upgrade the engine of the 500 from 140 HP to 160 HP, as well as its chassis, but re-homologation was required. During the year, the 695 Assetto Corse, another preview of the 695, came out. It replaced the 500 and had a 205 HP engine; and, since it was destined for racing, it was not homologated. It had special aerodynamic attachments and a 6-speed sequential gearbox. In 2013, the 50th anniversary of the original 595 was celebrated with a limited version (299 units plus 99 for Japan) called the 50th Anniversario, available only with the 695's 180 HP engine, automatic transmission, an enhanced braking system, an openable Skydome roof, and red and white leather interior.

180-181 JUST AS IN THE 60S, THE 595 WAS THE FIRST STEP WITH WHICH THE ABARTHS BROKE AWAY FROM THE SERIES. THE BASIC 140 HP CUSTOM SERIES COULD BE UPGRADED TO THE 160 HP OF THE TURISMO MODEL WITH A KIT THAT ALSO REQUIRED SUSPENSION ADJUSTMENTS AND RE-HOMOLOGATION. THE 595 OF THE ASSETTO CORSE DELIVERED 205 HP; IT WAS LIMITED TO USE ON THE RACETRACK.

ANYTHING BUT STANDARD: ABARTH 695 (2012)

In 2012, the 695 was rolled out. It was the last name of the Abarth 500s that had yet to be reutilized, except for the Tributo Ferrari version. There was no normal version equivalent to the Custom 500 or 595; only special series were produced. The first series of 499 units based on the 500C was dedicated to the Maserati brand. It was painted Pontevecchio Burgundy, one of the iconic colors of the Maserati Granturismo, with a beige leather interior, carbon details, and a JBL audio system.

The Record Grey Edition, launched in Frankfurt, was a limited edition of 49 units which came with a set of slate gray suitcases upon request. The recurring number 49 in the numbers of units produced is a reference to the year 1949, when Abarth was founded. The Maserati Edition debuted at the starting line of the reenactment of the Mille Miglia race. Its exhaust, called the Record Modena, was identical to the Record Monza except for the tips, which were redesigned to look like those of the Maserati Granturismo. The 695 Fuoriserie was presented at the Paris Motor Show with the name of Abarth & Co. appearing as the primary owner on the factory certificate. The Olio Fiat was the first special edition, painted the dark blue and yellow of the Fiat Lubrificanti oil cans of the 1960s that would become the colors of the victorious Fiat 131 Abarth at the end of the decade. The Abarth Brembo Koni kit available for the 695 was along the lines of the Esseesse kit for the 500 and 595. It included 17" wheels; drilled, self-ventilated front disc brakes; a 160 HP engine control unit; Eibach springs; and Koni shocks. Cars elaborated with the kit had to be re-homologated. In 2013, the Fuoriserie Edition added the collection New Wave, comprised of four versions: Record, Scorpione, Hype, and Black Diamond.

182 LEFT THE CABRIO 695 EDIZIONE MASERATI WAS AVAILABLE IN THE SAME COLORS (SUCH AS BORDEAUX PONTEVECCHIO), AND WITH THE SAME DETAILS, AS THE TRIDENTE GT.

182 RIGHT THE CABRIO 695 EDIZIONE MASERATI HAD THE SAME INTEGRATED HEADRESTS AS THE OTHER SPORTING MODELS AND SOFT CREAM-COLORED LEATHER SEATS.

183 A BODY KIT THAT GAVE THE 695 BIPOSTO AN EVEN FIERCER LOOK THAN THE OTHER ABARTHS WAS MADE BY THE GERMAN COMPANY ZENDER, USING A DESIGN BY ABARTH.

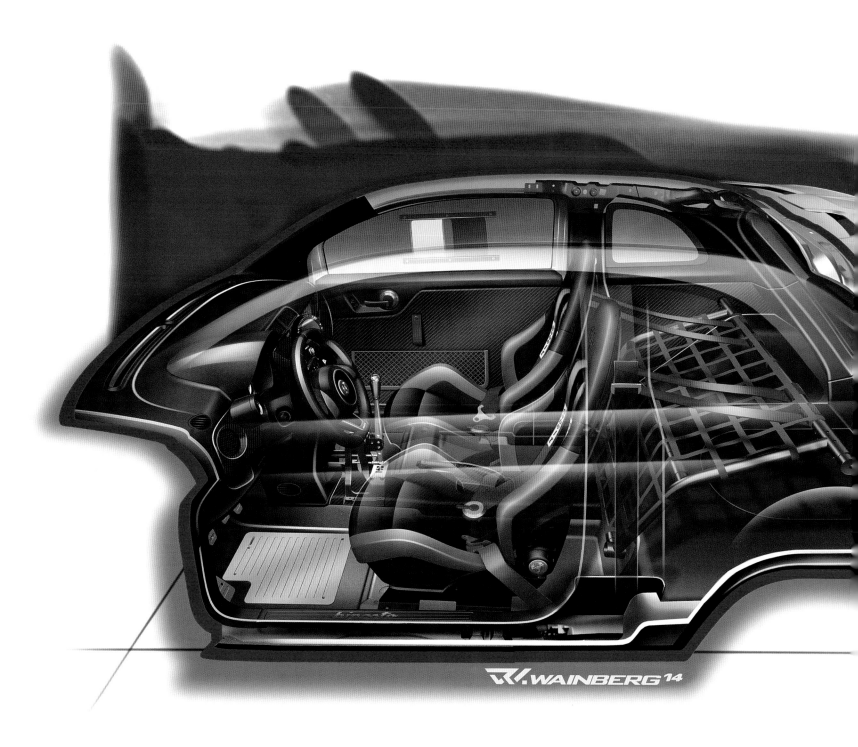

WAINBERG '14

March 2014 marked the creation of the 695 Two-Seater, the most extreme 500 ever to be produced (it could fly at 126 mph). Back seats were eliminated to make room for strut braces. It had a 190 HP engine with an intercooler and, on request, a dog ring gearbox made by Bacci that allows drivers with a good ear to change gears without using the clutch. It was loaded with racing components that included an Akrapovic exhaust, Sabelt racing seats, and a titanium roll bar by Poggipolini. It had 18" wheels and a telemetry system to analyze performance. ABS, ESP, and traction control were standard equipment, as were the self-locking differential and high performance friction discs. The car was homologated for the road, but it was undeniably a racecar; and to underline that fact, options such as a radio, air conditioning, power windows, fog lights, and Xenon headlights were not even available on demand. The body was styled with a kit produced by Zender from an Abarth design. It was painted a textured-effect matte gray, and the two bumps on the hood were reminiscent of the 124 Abarth from the '70s. The Biposto could be integrated with three kits: the 124 Special, Carbonio, and Pista, the last of which also included a technical racecar driver's suit. In September 2015, the Biposto Record, a special version of the Biposto, was presented at the International Motor Show in Frankfurt. 133 units were produced in yellow or gray, one for each record that the Abarth held.

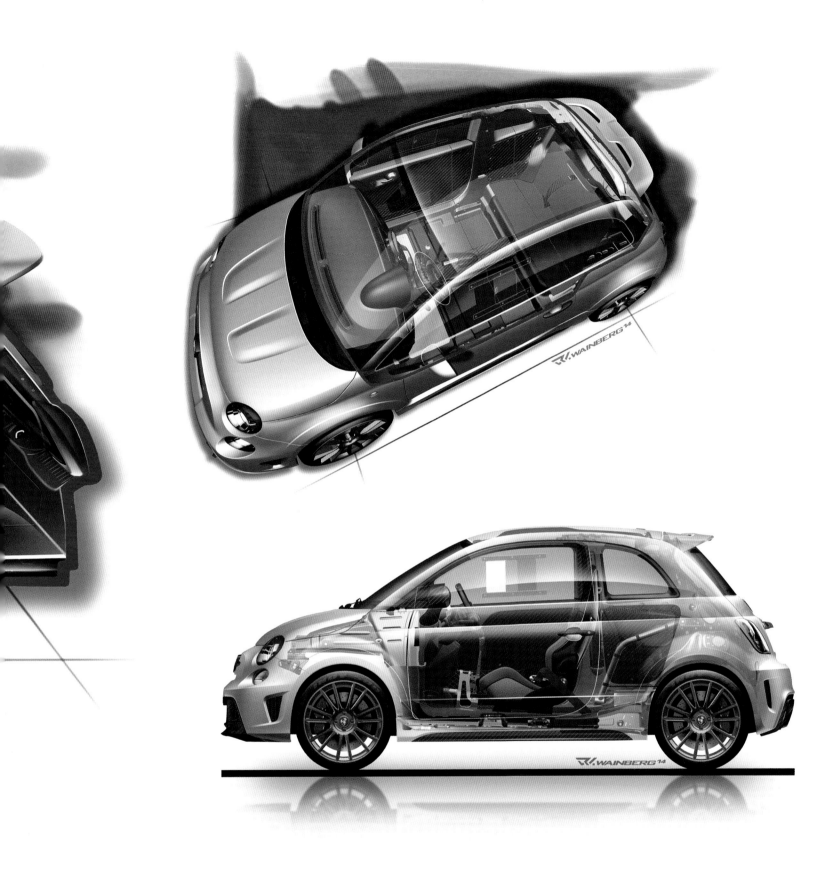

184-185 A TRANSPARENT VIEW OF THE INTERIOR OF THE 695 BIPOSTO SHOWS ITS SABELT SEATS AND STRUT BRACES. A DOG RING GEARBOX WAS OPTIONAL.

185 TOP A TRANSPARENT VIEW OF THE BIPOSTO WITH NO FRONT SEATS OR BRACES. THE DOUBLE-BUBBLE IN THE HOOD WAS PURELY ESTHETIC; IT WAS REMINISCENT OF THOSE OF THE 124 ABARTHS OF THE '70S.

185 BOTTOM A LATERAL TRANSPARENT VIEW OF THE BIPOSTO. DESPITE ITS EXTREME PERFORMANCE, THE ENGINE AND TRANSMISSION LAYOUT WERE THE SAME AS THOSE IN THE 500 IT DERIVED FROM.

EVERYTHING NEW AND NOTHING STANDARD: THE ABARTH 695 II SERIES (2016)

A restyling in 2016 introduced the same esthetic changes made to the 500 Fiat to the Abarth versions. With a turbine change in the 595 engine, the smooth-riding Turismo street car delivered 165 HP. The sportier Competizione, made for performance, delivered 180 HP and had the 695's Brembo brakes. There was also news from the 500 family at the 2017 Geneva Motor Show. It was the 595 Abarth Pista, powered by a 160 HP 1,400 cc engine, with special selective-damping Koni shock absorbers and a Record Monza exhaust system that could be opened up by the driver to get a more aggressive sound and closed for a more gentlemanly-sounding ride. It was available in white, gray, Abarth red, Record gray, and Scorpion black. The electronics on board included a telemetry system with maps of the most famous circuits in Europe. Models of the following years were characterized by a wider range of equipment, such as the Urban trim package that included rain sensors, light sensors, and parking sensors; and leather upholstered or Sabelt seats, depending on the model, became standard equipment. One of the new colors was Adrenaline green; it debuted in 2019 on the 595 Competizione and was the color of the details of the 2020 Pista's matte light gray body.

The Abarth 695 Yamaha XSR celebrated the renewed collaboration between Fiat and Valentino Rossi's motorcycle team. Created on the base of the 595 Pista, it was gray with exhausts designed by the specialist Akrapovic, and could be taken to 180 HP with a tuning kit. 695 sedans and 695 soft-tops were produced. The 70° Anniversario, a commemorative series of 1,949 units, was presented at the 2019 Abarth Days. Its 12-position adjustable spoiler was a distinguishing feature; it increased the downforce on the back axle and reduced the need to correct steering. Its Green Monza 1958 color was evocative of the Abarth 500 that set seven records in seven days in 1958. The engine was a 180 HP 1,400 cc turbo. In 2019, the Esseesse version came back with a 180 HP engine, Akrapovic exhaust, selective-damping Koni shocks, and a special air filter that improved air turbulence for better combustion. Sabelt racing seats and 17" wheels were standard equipment.

186-187 THE PRODUCTION OF THE 70TH ANNIVERSARY 695 WAS LIMITED TO 1,949 UNITS, IN HONOR OF THE YEAR THAT ABARTH WAS FOUNDED. IT WAS THE SAME COLOR GREEN AS THE NUOVA 500 ABARTH THAT SHATTERED SIX WORLD RECORDS IN MONZA.

THE 500 STARTS A FAMILY: THE 500 L I SERIES (2012–2017)

188-189 THE 500 L HAD SOME OF THE SAME ENGINES AND
TRANSMISSIONS AS THE 500, BUT IT HAD THE LARGER PLATFORM OF
THE GRANDE PUNTO, TO GUARANTEE MORE SPACE. IT WAS PRODUCED IN
KRAGUJEVAC, SERBIA.

In 2009, insistent talk began of the 500 as the FCA group's new brand, with models that were roomier joining the two-door models. Sketches of the new vehicles and photos of masked prototypes appeared in the specialized press, which was a bit confused about the future "big 500s" and the third series of Pandas. The 500's big sister, codenamed L0, reintroduced a historical Fiat acronym, just as the 500 C had done. It was announced in the 2010 business plan and presented in Geneva in February 2012. Sales began in July. Production began in April in the Serbian plant at Kragujevac where the Zastava models had been produced since 1953. FCA had bought the factory in 2008 and restructured it. The 500 L was immediately designated for the markets in Europe and North America (in May 2013), so it was designed to conform with the strict vehicle safety standards of the American NHTSA. The structure was constructed of high-strength steel and polymeric compounds. It was rolled out with the Fiat brand after having decided that the "500" was a product line with a strong identity, not a brand.

The bed came from the same family as that of the Doblò van and the Grande Punto. The 500 L was proposed in two lengths; the basic and Trekking versions were shorter at 161.4 inches (4,100 mm); the Trekking was 5.9 inches (150 mm) taller; while the Living, which went on the market in June 2013, was longer at 171.2 inches (4,350 mm). The wheelbases of the two models were identical so they could be manufactured using the same doors. The extra length was in the overhang, which made it possible to put two additional seats in the back, like in big American station wagons. There were four trim packages available: Pop, Pop Star, Easy, and Lounge. The gasoline engines were the 105 HP Twinair 90 and the 94 HP Fire 1,400 cc, and the diesel engine was the 95 HP Multijet 1,300 cc. Fiat described the 500 L as "cool and capable," a good indication that the target audience was one that cared about looks as much as about practicality. The new model replaced the smaller Idea as well as the larger Multipla; its design, which was vintage but less audacious than the Multipla, won over drivers from the category of mid-size sedans like the Bravo, a category that had no station wagon. A version with a glass Skydome roof went on sale in December 2012.

The 500 Ls powered by gasoline engines were available with a 105 HP Twinair 900 cc, a 95 HP Fire 1,400 cc (in 2013), a 120 HP T-jet 1,400 cc, and, for the U.S. market, a 165 HP Multiair 1,400 cc. The LPG version of the 85 HP Twinair came out in 2013, the same year that the 105 HP and 120 HP Multijet were made available in addition to the initial 85 HP Multijet diesel.

In October 2013, other engine options were added with the 80 HP Twinair 900 cc turbo, both gasoline and LPG and the 120 HP Multijet diesel. In December 2013, the 120 HP T-Jet 1,400 cc debuted in all three versions. In 2013, the basic version became the Urban and the Pro was introduced, a five-seater homologated as a category N1 truck.

NEW IN THE FAMILY: 500L II SERIES (SINCE 2017)

In 2017, the 500 L also got a facelift. Like the restyling of the normal 500, it updated its look, to make it fresher and more modern, without denaturing it. At the Bologna Motor Show in November, the Trekking made way for the Cross, which had a higher ride, skid plates, and a traction mode selector with Normal, Traction+ for slippery surfaces, and Gravity Control for downhill driving. The name of the Urban remained unchanged, while the Living was renamed the Wagon. In February 2018, the 500,000th 500 L rolled off the line in Serbia. The year 2020 offered a basic version, two Cross models (the Cross and the Sport), and the Wagon, which was available in the Urban or Lounge versions—in addition to the Business version, which was destined for car fleets. The gasoline engine was a 95 HP Fire 1,400 cc, and the diesel engines were a 95 HP Multijet II 1,300 cc with an automatic transmission and a 120 HP 1,600 cc.

190   THE COLOR BLACK ALSO CHARACTERIZED THE INTERIOR OF THE 500 L S-DESIGN, FROM THE UPHOLSTERY TO THE DASHBOARD AND DOOR COVERINGS.

190-191   WITH ITS BLACK DETAILS, THE S-DESIGN GAVE A BOLD TOUCH TO THE CITY CROSS, THE HIGH RIDING VERSION OF THE 500 L. THE 500 X AND THE TIPO ALSO HAD THE SAME LINE OF DETAILS, WHICH WAS CREATED IN 2019.

In December 2017, the Mirror version was also launched for the 500 L. It descended from the basic version and had a screen that displayed the functions of the infotainment system as well as the apps and contents of the driver's smartphone. It was produced in two special colors, Blue Venice and Gray Maestro.

The S-Design, a descendant of the City Cross, was presented in January 2019. It was available with a Fire 1,400 cc gasoline engine or a Multijet II 1,300 cc or 1,600 cc diesel engine. It was matte bronze with black or burnished Myron accents. A second series followed in 2019 in Alpine green. The 120th Anniversary version, also offered in the 500, 500 C and 500 X, was launched at the Geneva Motor Show in March 2019, in a two-toned, black and white Tuxedo livery. It came with a Mopar Connect platform that also provided vehicle health reports.

192 AT THE TOP, THE CROSS VERSION, WITH A RAISED RIDE, PLATES UNDER THE BUMPERS, AND TRACTION CONTROL FOR DRIVING DOWNHILL OR ON SLIPPERY SURFACES.

193 TOP THE VERSION WITH A LONGER REAR OVERHANG CAN SEAT SEVEN. IN THE SECOND SERIES, IT WAS CALLED WAGON.

192-193 THE SPECIAL LIMITED SERIES THAT COMMEMORATED FIAT'S 120TH ANNIVERSARY IN TWO-TONED TUXEDO WHITE.

HERE COMES THE 4X4: 500X I SERIES (SINCE 2015)

The design for the 500 X drew more inspiration from the Nuova 500 than the 500 L had. The 500X was a midsize SUV that competed in the C segment, despite having been created on a small bed, like the L. It was constructed in the Melfi factory in the Basilicata region, on the same bed as the Jeep Renegade. It was announced in Paris in 2014 and was put on the market in January 2015. The first series included the City Look, destined for urban driving and available only with two-wheel drive, and the Off-Road Look, with two- or four-wheel drive. Like the L, it was immediately ready for the American market. The design is that of a "pumped-up" 500, with a taller and more muscular body. The Off-Road Look versions had bumper protection plates. They were initially proposed with a 140 HP Multiair 1,400 cc gasoline engine and a 120 HP Multijet II 1,600-cc and 140 HP Multijet II 2,000-cc diesel engines (the 2,000 cc was available only in the Cross version). The 170 HP Multiair and the 120 HP T-Jet Easypower 1,400 cc, both gasoline and LPG versions, were added to the engine choices in 2016 and 2017 respectively. In October 2016, the option of an automatic 6-speed transmission with dual clutch was added to the already available 6-speed manual transmission and the 9-speed automatic, which is uncommon in this category.

198 A SKETCH FROM THE CENTRO STILE FIAT THAT HIGHLIGHTS THE X'S MUSCLE. THE NEW
TAILLIGHT GROUPS HAD AN INSERT THAT MATCHED THE BODY COLOR, LIKE THE 500 II SERIES.

199 THE FRONT END ALSO GOT NEW FEATURES THAT WERE REMINISCENT OF THE LITTLE 500
THREE-DOOR, INCLUDING HORIZONTAL LED PARKING LIGHTS.

The 500s as Masterpieces

The 500 had its first encounter with art through the patronage that led many big industries to commission works of art from well-known and emerging artists in the first half of the 20th century.

Defined as a design masterpiece, a pop icon, an ambassador of Italian style, each version of the little Fiat continues to inspire all kinds of art: paintings, sculptures, and, of course, movies, where the car has played "live" roles as well as the animated roles that have brought it international fame in the world of cinema. One of the first big names to depict the 500 was Mario Sironi, a painter who at the time of the Topolino had abandoned pointillism and futurism for the neoclassicism and metaphysics of de Chirico and Carrà. His 500, painted with the fresco technique and depicted with the Capitoline Wolf in the background, evokes the "Italianism" that was so beloved by the fascist regime. The same car in movement, a theme that futurists loved, also exuded propaganda. The car is depicted as it travels over a background that is a cubist painting of Italy with a network of major roads traced on it. Strangely, that version of Italy included Corsica.

THE CAPITOLINE WOLF WITH ROMULUS AND REMUS WAS A RECURRING ELEMENT IN THE SOCIAL-IDENTITY CULTURE DURING ITALY'S PERIOD OF FASCISM. HERE SHE IS PORTRAYED WITH THE 500, "A PRODUCT OF ITALY'S GENIUS," IN AN ILLUSTRATION BY MARIO SIRONI.

ANOTHER ILLUSTRATION BY MARIO SIRONI DEPICTS A 500, DEFORMED BY SPEED AND READY TO RACE THROUGH A RATHER FANCIFUL NETWORK OF HIGHWAYS.

FIAT
500

The painter, engraver, and decorator Attilio Corsetti also portrayed the Topolino. In his poster, he used a combined technique of divisionism and stencil to depict a side view of the car in front of a globe as it travels upward along a road of a metaphysical city with rationalistic architecture.

The posters by Nico Edel, a Swiss artist who studied in Turin, used clean-cut lines and bold, uniform colors to evoke practicality and speed. The only reference to the regime was the eagle in the background of one of the posters that claimed that the 500 was "the economy car that conquered the world." Edel's 500s appear to be deformed by speed, which made them appear so long and low that they looked like the 1500.

Although he had had a significant career as a landscape artist with a strong, substantial brushstroke, the style of Felice Vellan's ink drawings was that of an illustrator, ironic and empathetic with his subjects. The drawings, which were destined for a magazine, portrayed the Topolino on a golf course and on the ski slopes of Sestriere, where athletes and passengers on a Fiat 635 bus admired it with envy and curiosity.

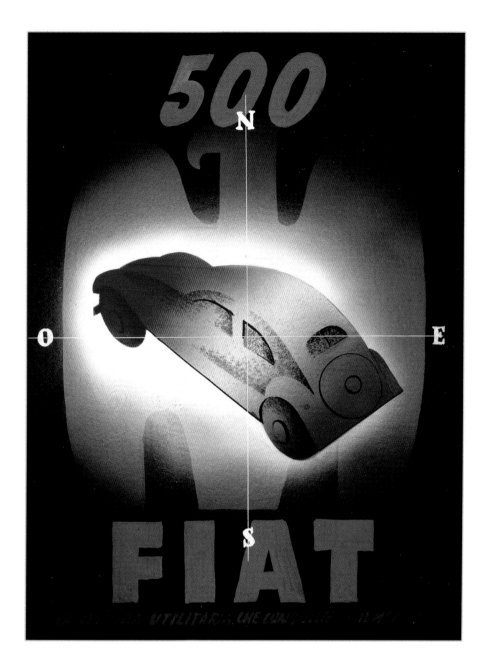

202 ATTILIO CORSETTI'S 500 OWES MUCH TO THE COLORS OF FUTURISTS LIKE BALLA AND DEPERO; THE CITY IN THE BACKGROUND, TO METAPHYSICAL PAINTING. IT WAS THE FIRST TIME THAT "500" WAS WRITTEN WITH A LONG "5."

203 TOP IN AN ILLUSTRATION BY NICO EDEL, A PURE WHITE LIGHT SHINING FROM BELOW ILLUMINATES THE 500 AS IT REFLECTS THE THREE COLORS OF THE ITALIAN FLAG. IN THE BACKGROUND IS AN ALMOST-CONCEALED FASCIST EAGLE.

203 BOTTOM IN FELICE VELLAN'S INK DRAWING, THE 500 SEEMS EVEN SMALLER THAN IT ACTUALLY WAS, BUT THAT DID NOT MAKE THE PASSENGERS ON THE BUS DESIRE IT ANY LESS.

204 THE 500 IN NICO EDEL'S ILLUSTRATION SEEMS TO BE DEFORMED BY SPEED, AN INSPIRATION THAT FUTURISTS LOVED BUT THAT TODAY IS DIFFICULT TO RELATE TO THE 500'S MEDIOCRE PERFORMANCE. IN THE ITALY OF THE 1930S, SIMPLY HAVING A MOTOR WOULD GIVE YOUR LIFE A BURST OF SPEED IT HAD NEVER HAD BEFORE.

205 ANOTHER STREAMLINED 500 BY EDEL, WITH ITS HEADLIGHTS CURIOUSLY MOUNTED ON THE FENDER ARCHES, LIKE ON GIACOSA'S SECOND PROTOTYPE. PORTRAYING THE TOPOLINO WITH A BUSINESSMAN WHO USED IT TO TRAVEL FOR WORK PERFECTLY CONVEYED THE SPIRIT OF THE UTILITY CAR THAT IT WAS DESIGNED TO BE.

206 A POSTER BY BECCARIA, AN ILLUSTRATOR WHO WORKED IN FIAT'S COMMUNICATIONS OFFICE, FOR THE 500 MATCH, A SERIES OF PRIZE COMPETITION REGULARITY RACES ORGANIZED BY THE ROME AUTOMOBILE CLUB IN 1958.

207 ANOTHER POSTER FOR THE 500 MATCH. THIS ONE BY NINO AIMONE, A PAINTER FROM TURIN WHO STUDIED UNDER FELICE CASORATI. HE WORKED IN FIAT'S COMMUNICATIONS OFFICE UNTIL THE EARLY 1970S.

Portraits of the 500 "model 110" were the fruit of an era in which an industry's patronage for the arts was no longer tied to its products. The works of art decorated corporate headquarters and offices; the names of the sponsors on posters for exhibits were minuscule. Photos began being used as images in advertising. Artists were called on to illustrate institutional publications and greeting cards. Nino Aimone, who was employed in Fiat's propaganda office at the time, used colored ink to create a card that portrayed the 500 Giardiniera in a northern European village, and Antonio Zoffili used temperas to depict the Nuova 500 in the snow in traffic in Turin, with Piazza San Carlo and a mother and child doing Christmas shopping.

208 THE SHADE OF BLUE AND THE HALF-TIMBERED HOUSES ARE REMINISCENT OF NORTHERN EUROPE, BUT BOTH THE ARTIST AND THE SUBJECT OF THIS CHRISTMAS ILLUSTRATION ARE FULL-BLOODED ITALIAN: NINO AIMONE AND THE 500 GIARDINIERA.

209 THE TURIN OF ANTONIO ZOFFILI'S ILLUSTRATION IS WRAPPED IN THE CHRISTMAS SPIRIT: A MOTHER AND CHILD WALK TOWARD THEIR 500 PARKED UNDER THE CAVAL ËD BRONS, THE EQUESTRIAN MONUMENT DEDICATED TO THE DUKE OF SAVOY, EMANUELE FILIBERTO, IN PIAZZA SAN CARLO.

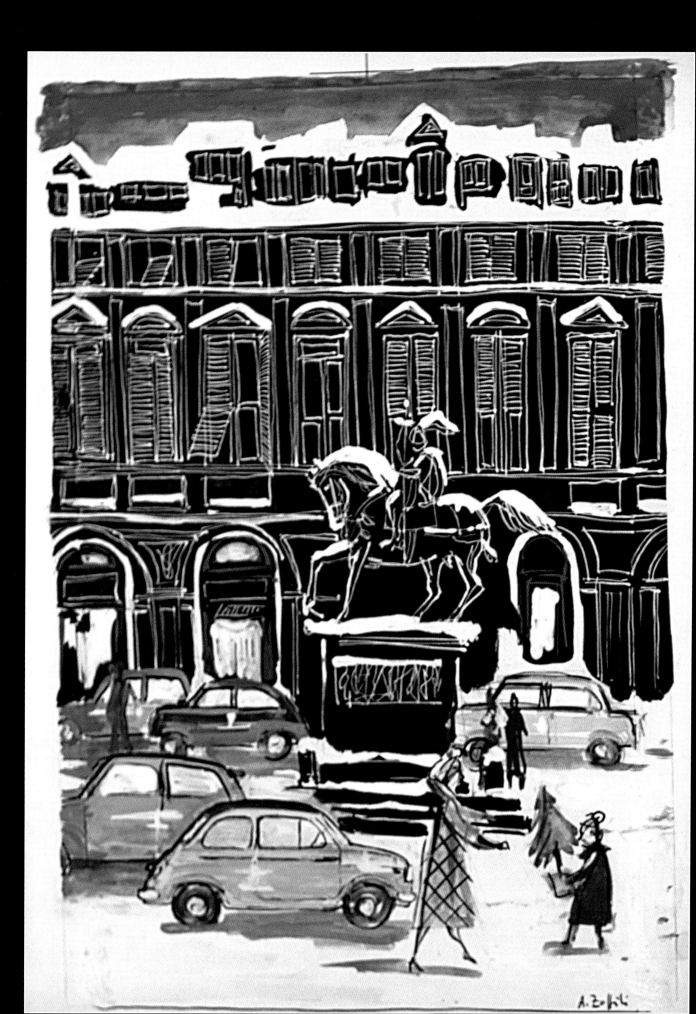

A 2007 model 500 was stylized and painted in bold colors in an array of combinations by the cross-disciplinary artist from Pavia, Marco Lodola. He used two of his classic techniques, the luminous sericollage and the rectangular or molded luminous box, reproduced in screen-printing. He used the same vivacious colors to depict the 500 L.

"Why Africa" was one of the very first new-generation 500s painted by the South African artist Esther Mahlangu with traditional motifs of the Ndebele tribe.

The car was displayed in the "Why Africa" exhibit at the Gianni and Marella Agnelli museum in Turin and was auctioned at the charity event Convivio Milano, which raises funds for the battle against AIDS. In the 1980s, Mahlangu painted a BMW 5 series with the same tribal motifs.

210-211 ESTHER MAHLANGU ON THE ROOF OF THE LINGOTTO FACTORY WITH HER "WHY AFRICA?," A PAINTED 2007 MODEL 500 THAT WAS AUCTIONED TO COLLECT FUNDS IN THE BATTLE AGAINST AIDS.

Sculptures of the 500 began with the vintage models that played the role of automobile archetypes in the era in which they were created. Arman (Pierre Fernandez) from Nice uses technical virtuosity to produce highly detailed ceramic objects that are normally made from completely different materials, such as car motors. In 1994, he reproduced a black-and-amaranth-colored skeleton of a 500 C with a cascade of teapots that fall from the car. Arman poses the issue of what is real and what is false in art, and everything in his work is contrived—not just the 500 C but also the teapots, which were reproductions made for the installation.

212-213 EVERYTHING IN THE CERAMIC WORK OF THE FRENCH ARTIST ARMAN IS FICTITIOUS, FROM THE PRECISELY DETAILED LIFE-SIZE 500 C TO THE TEAPOTS THAT SPILL OUT OF ITS INTERIOR AS THOUGH IT WERE A HORN OF PLENTY.

The Israeli architect and designer Ron Arad lives and works in London. He designed the Bookworm bookcase for Kartell; and in 2013 he produced the "Pressed Flower" series with six 500 Fs and 500 Ls. The cars were flattened, exactly as if they were flowers between the pages of a book, using a process that would allow them to keep their appearance and definition. Mechanical parts, interiors, and anything that would hinder the flattening process were removed from the cars, and parts that might have broken during the process, such as door handles and headlights, were disassembled and then remounted when the crushing was complete. Arad also created the "Roddy Giacosa," a life-size sculpture of a 500 created with steel tubing, and "Slow Outburst," a video that simulates the compression of a recent-model Fiat 500. He also designed a series of 1:1-ratio adhesives that, when applied to the sides of the 2007 model of the 500, reproduced the lines of the model 110. The resulting 500 was sold as the "Ron Arad Edition."

214-215 ISRAELI ARCHITECT AND DESIGNER RON ARAD DEDICATED A NUMBER OF ARTWORKS TO DANTE GIACOSA AND HIS CREATIONS. "PRESSED FLOWERS" IS A SERIES OF FIVE 500S FROM THE L TO THE F AT THE END OF THEIR CAREERS. THE CARS WERE SOURCED IN GREAT BRITAIN AND THEN CRUSHED, JUST AS FLOWERS ARE PRESSED BETWEEN THE PAGES OF A BOOK, IN SUCH A WAY AS TO PRESERVE THEIR FEATURES. THE SERIES WAS DISPLAYED AT THE LINGOTTO'S GIANNI AND MARELLA AGNELLI GALLERY IN 2013.

In 2011, Lorenzo Quinn, son of the actor Anthony Quinn, created an installation called *Vroom Vroom*, a 13-foot-tall (4 m) steel hand grasping a dark blue 500 L in a gesture that recalls a child playing with a toy car. It has been displayed in London, Valencia, and Abu Dhabi.

The Salvator Rosa subway station in Naples is home to an installation created by Emiliano Perino and Luca Vele titled *À subway è cchiù sicura,* meaning "the subway is safer." The installation is made of scrapped 500 bodies, draped with quilts to call attention to the fact that using public transportation is safer than using a private vehicle.

216-217 THE GESTURE IS THAT OF A SMALL CHILD PUSHING A MODEL CAR, BUT THE ENORMOUS HAND IS ACTUALLY 46 FEET (14 M) TALL AND THE 500 L IS REAL. THE WORK, BY LORENZO QUINN, IS CALLED "VROOM VROOM."

It would be impossible to list all the movies and television shows that the 500 and its derivatives appear in. The *Internet Movie Cars Database* website (imcdb.org) reports more than 5,000 appearances of the 500, Bianchina, 126, Cinquecento, and Seicento. Every popular Italian movie from the '60s and '70s has at least one, in roles of varying importance. Many were demolished during the filming of police movie chases in the '70s, along with big foreign sedans that were hard to resell. Italian comedies often included the ironic role of the "if I could afford something better, I would" kind of car, beginning with the *Fantozzi series* starring Paolo Villaggio with his Bianchina sedan, and *James Tont Operazione U.N.O.*, a parody of a James Bond movie in which the star, Lando Buzzanca, drives a first-series 500 F instead of an Aston Martin. The 500 appears in such art films as Pierpaolo Pasollni's *Teorema* and *Mamma Roma* as well as in François Truffaut's *Day for Night*. A 500 D and a Bianchina convertible appeared in *The Pink Panther,* an American production filmed in Italy by Blake Edwards. The car probably had its best role in Billy Wilder's 1972 movie *Avanti!,* starring Jack Lemmon and Juliet Mills. A run-down 500 D whizzes around the streets of Ischia, driven by the Trotta brothers who represent the typical international stereotype of Italians, cheaters and opportunists who aren't really all that bad at heart.

The charming shape of the Tipo 110 500 was a favorite in cartoons. The cartoon characters who drove a 500 include Lupin III, a comic book character inspired by Arsène Lupin, the gentleman thief created by the writer Maurice Leblanc. Lupin III was drawn by the Japanese Monkey Punch in 1967 and then made into a cartoon in 1972. The Nuova 500 was the perfect car for Lupin, but he often drove a 1930s Mercedes SSK or a Morgan 4/4. In recent episodes, he appeared in a 2007 model of the 500.

Just as famous is Luigi, the owner of the tire shop in the three Disney-Pixar movies in the *Cars* series, who encourages the growth and career of the racecar Lightning McQueen. Luigi is a yellow Nuova 500 who loves racecars and is a fan of the Ferrari. Like all the characters in the movie, he is humanized rather than anthropomorphous, with eyes in place of the windshield and a grill that moves like a mouth.

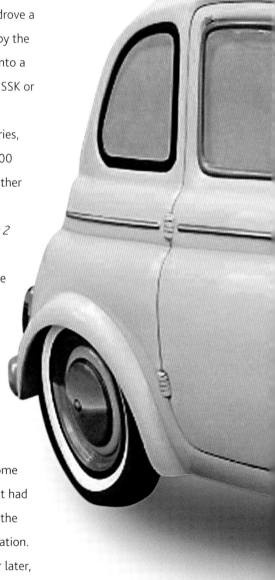

Lucy, the secret agent who becomes the new girlfriend of Gru, the head minion in *Despicable Me 2* (2013, directed by Pierre Coffin and Chris Renaud), drives a Bianchina. The historical 500 made a number of appearances in *Family Guy,* which came out in 1999, and a 500 was seen in more than one episode of the Japanese cartoon, *Dragonball*.

The 500 has often been the subject or the background in photographs, particularly those taken by photographers dedicated to traditions, social comment, and news reporting. The Fiat economy car was an essential component in the narration of the three decades in which Italians went from an economic boom to the dark years of terrorism and to the first effects of deindustrialization. One 500 with a particular history was the C that belonged to the Dutch photographer Erik Kessels. He used the car to tell the story of his relationship with his father, a scrupulous restorer of Topolinos whose work was interrupted when he had a stroke. Kessels chose some shots that his father used to document his restorations and used them, together with a car body that had been restored and was ready to be remounted, to create the installation titled *The unfinished father,* the story of a man who, after having a stroke, was to remain forever "unfinished," just like his last restoration. Kessels presented his work at the 2015 edition of European Photography in Reggio Emilia and, a year later, at the Deutsche Börse Photography Foundation Prize, where he was among the finalists. The car body was displayed, hanging from a steel cable, outside the Photographers' Gallery in Soho, London.

218-219 LUIGI IS THE OWNER OF THE TIRE SHOP IN RADIATOR SPRINGS, A VILLAGE INHABITED BY TALKING (AND THINKING) CARS. HE FIXES TIRES AND IS FRIEND AND CONFIDANT TO THE RACECAR CHAMPION LIGHTNING MCQUEEN.

219 AN ADVERTISING INSTALLATION CELEBRATES LUPIN III AND HIS FAITHFUL PARTNER DAISUKE JIGEN, CHARACTERS OF THE MONKEY PUNCH MANGA, AND THEIR MOST FAMOUS CAR, THE 500.

220–221 THE FRAME AND BODY OF A PARTIALLY RESTORED 500 HANGING OUTSIDE THE PHOTOGRAPHER'S GALLERY IN SOHO, LONDON DURING ERIK KESSELS'S EXHIBIT, "UNFINISHED FATHER." THE PROJECT USED THE INTERRUPTED RESTORATION WORK OF KESSELS'S OWN FATHER, A RESTORER OF TOPOLINOS WHO HAD HAD A STROKE, TO TELL THE STORY OF HIS INTERRUPTED LIFE.

Author

MASSIMO CONDOLO was born in Turin in 1968 and lives in the province of Milan. He studied at the Polytechnic University of Turin. At a very young age, he began his career in technical communications in the transportation systems and automotive industry sectors, first as a press agent and then as a journalist and author of books about the history of road and rail transportation. He works as a test driver of cars and heavy vehicles and as a technical instructor in the automotive field (he collaborated to design and create the first course for experts in the field of classic and collector cars, among other things). He works with a number of publications, including *Tuttotrasporti.* In the past, he put together, restored, and maintained fleets of historic buses, trucks, trams, and trains for "live" museum displays that showed these vehicles in use.

Aknowledgments

For the materials that they kindly contributed to the collection of images in this volume, the editor wishes to thank the Fiat Historical Center, FCA Heritage Hub, Fondazione Negri, Topolino Autoclub Italia, and Registro Autobianchi.

For their precious collaboration, Massimo Condolo wishes to thank Fabio Alberani, Massimo Castagnola, Riccardo Gorni, Umberto Fabrizio Hardouin, Marco Lerda, Laura Lodi, Pierangela Piazza, Jonny Porcu, Roberto Righi, and Alberta Simonis.

Photo Credits

Project Editor VALERIA MANFERTO DE FABIANIS

Editorial assistants GIORGIA RAINERI AND GIORGIO FERRERO

Graphic Designer PAOLA PIACCO

WS White Star Publishers® is a registered trademark property of White Star s.r.l.

© 2021 White Star s.r.l.
Piazzale Luigi Cadorna, 6
20123 Milan, Italy
www.whitestar.it

ISBN 978-88-544-1715-1
1 2 3 4 5 6   25 24 23 22 21

Printed in Croatia

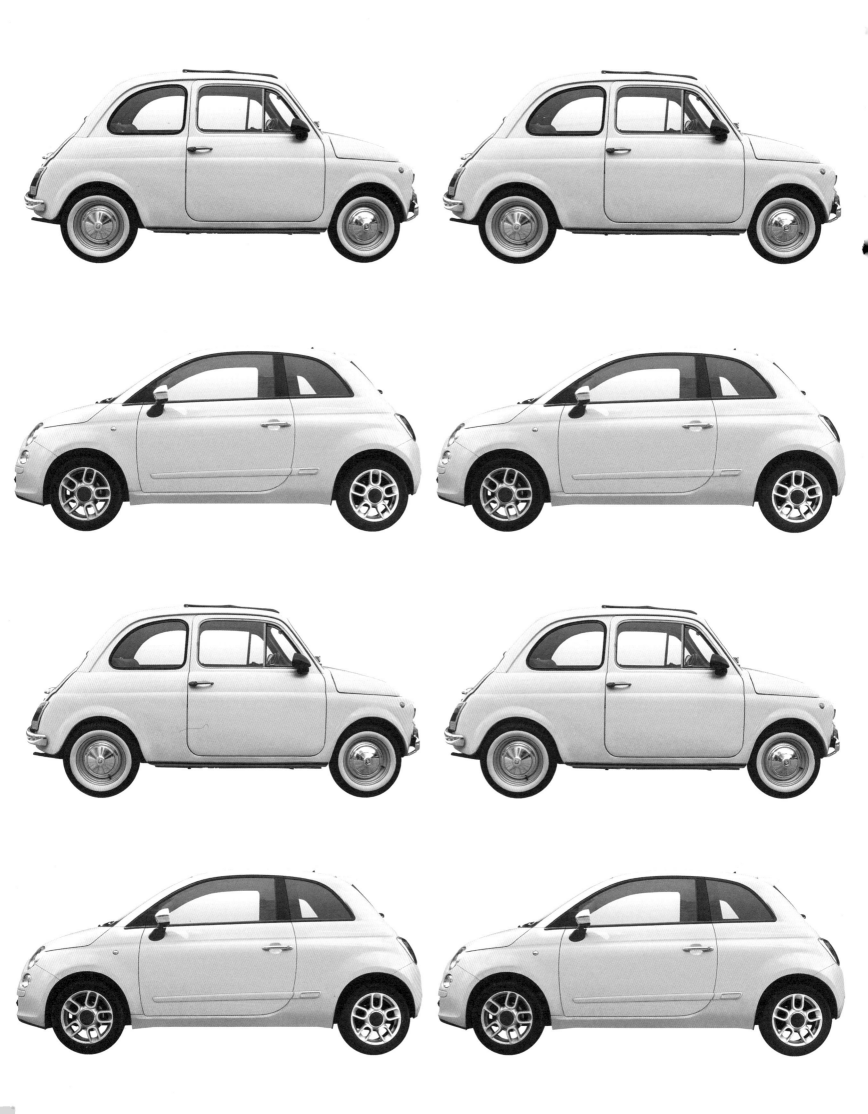